PYROPHORIC ZEN

FURTHER ZEN RAMBLINGS FROM THE INTERNET

SCOTT SHAW

BUDDHA ROSE PUBLICATIONS

Pyrophoric Zen
Further Zen Ramblings from the Internet
Copyright © 2018 by Scott Shaw
www.scottshaw.com\J
ALL RIGHTS RESERVED

Cover photographs by Scott Shaw.

Rear cover photograph of Scott Shaw
by Hae Won Shin.

First Edition 2018

ISBN 10: 1-949251-09-8
ISBN 13: 978-1-949251-09-8

Library of Congress: 2018965514

10 9 8 7 6 5 4 3 2 1
Printed in the United States of America

PYROPHORIC
ZEN

Introduction

Here it is, *The Scott Shaw Zen Blog 12.0,* originally presented on the World Wide Web. All of the writings presented in this book were written between May and August of 2018.

As was the case with the previously published volumes based upon *The Scott Shaw Zen Blog;* entitled: *Scribbles on the Restroom Wall, The Chronicles: Zen Ramblings from the Internet, Words in the Wind, Zen Mind Life Thoughts, The Zen of Life, Lies, and Aberrant Reality, Apostrophe Zen, and The Abstract Arsenal of Zen and the Psychology of Being, Zen and Again: The Metaphysical Philosophy of Psychology, Tempest in a Teapot and the Den of Zen, Buddha in the Looking Glass, Wo Ton' of the Blue Vision,* and *Zen and the Psychology of the Spiritual Something,* this volume is presented exactly as it was viewed on scottshaw.com with no rewriting, punctuation, or typo corrections. From this, we hope you will receive the original reading experience.

This volume of internet ramblings is presented with the date and time listed as to when each blog was originally posted. Also, the blogs in this volume are presented from last to first. With this, we hope to present a transcendence back through time as opposed to an evolving evolution. In addition, we left out the traditional *Table of Contents* in an attempt to leave this volume with a much more free-flowing reading experience.

Okay, there's the information and the definitions. Read on… We hope you enjoy it. And, be sure to stayed tuned for the ongoing *Scott Shaw Zen Blog* @ scottshaw.com.

Fade In:

*   *   *

14/Aug/2018 12:15 PM

If you are sitting around concentrating on what someone else is doing that means you are doing nothing with your own life.

Do You Care?
14/Aug/2018 08:25 AM

There are people who are hurting all over the world. Some of these hurts are massive life altering events. There are people who are trapped in war zones or surrounded by famine and disease. Then there are people who have been attacked and have had their lives and/or their psyche damaged or ruined by what other people have done to them. There are also people who are hurting due to small things. The motivating factors for their hurt are so many it would be impossible to list them all but maybe it is something so seemingly minor as loneliness or not having enough money to buy something that they want and believe that they need. Yet, none-the-less, from this absence of something they still feel internal pain. But, here is the question... ...Here comes the defining factor of your life. Do you care?

A person's life is defined by how they think. A person's life is defined by how they act towards others defined by how they think. How do you think? What does how you think cause you to do? How does what you think cause you to think about others and how does what you think cause you to do the things you do towards others?

If you look at your life you will quickly see that who you are right now, in this moment of time, has been largely affected by the way other people have treated you. Yes, of course, you have personality and you hold personal choice about how you choose to behave if you choose to possess the mental wherewithal to be in control of your thinking mind. But, for most people, they live a life based upon a reactive consciousness formulated upon how they have been schooled to behave by the actions of others. From this, they do actions to others. And, from that, other people's lives are shaped. Thus, you are responsible for the emotions and the life experiences of others. Do you ever think about that? Most people don't.

Some people, whether knowingly or not, revel in this power that they possess. Bosses and people in positions of authority quite commonly allow this mindset to take control over their entire being. Others choose to dominate people by fear. While others simply only think about themselves and they do not care about how what they are doing is affecting the life of any other person as long as they are obtaining what they want.

Look around yourself; these patterns of behavior are very prevalent. Look to yourself, how do you behave towards others? Study your actions and your reactions. Now, take a moment and analyze what people have done to you that has affected the way you behave towards other people. Where do you find the place of your personality instigation and stimulus in all of this?

To take this personality study a bit farther, have you ever had somebody do something to you that hurt you? How did that person behave after they did that something?

We need to make something very clear at this point in the discussion. Most people base all of their emotions solely upon on how they feel. They do not take the other person in the equitation into consideration at all. Thus, it is essential that when you look at this process you do not simply study how you feel about how a person reacted to something you instigated. If you started it, that something is your fault. How a person reacted is simply their reaction but they are not the causation factor. You are. Thus, they are simply the reactive factor and you cannot judge them for that reaction.

Back to the question: somebody hurt you; what did that person do after the fact?

In some cases people will say, *"Sorry."* But, do they mean it? If they even care enough to express sorrow that is a step in the right direction. But, most use the term, *"Sorry,"* simply as a fix-all Band-Aid but that word does nothing at all.

First of all, if a person has the consciousness to care they probably would not have done what they did to you in the first place. If they did mistakenly do something they would then set about on a course to repair the hurt they inflicted. But, how many people do that? Very few. Do you?

Here, we are brought to the essence of all of the pain in the world. Do you care? Do you care enough to care? Can you care? Can you care enough to care to not do something that will hurt somebody else? And, if you do something that hurts someone else, can you care enough to care to put your own desires, ego, and mind-stuff on hold long enough to repair what you have done? Moreover, can you care about the people that are hurting out there? The people you have never met? The people who are hurting because of nothing you have personally done? Or, have you?

Like I express over-and-over again, all of the world begins with you. What you do spreads outwards and affects everyone. The food you eat causes someone to feel pain. Where and how you live causes someone to feel pain. What you choose to do obviously has the potential to cause other people pain. So yes, though you may live in denial about the fact, you are responsible for the everything. Do you care? And, what are you going to do about it?

Caring begins with small things. It begins by caring about others. It begins by caring enough to not to do something that has the potential to hurt someone else. It begins by fixing what you have broken. It begins by putting what you want on hold and thinking about the other person first. Again, do you care? And, can you care enough to care?

Gotta Keep Punchin'
AKA Blood is Thicker Than Water
13/Aug/2018 08:56 AM

I was watching this episodic TV show last week where one of the central characters got mugged. Earlier that evening I was watching a reality TV show where two main groups had split from a central business they worked at and had become warring factions. They two groups both arrived at a location and a fight broke out. But, on the two sides were two brothers who refused to become part of the melee, stating I would never attack my brother. All of this sent me to thinking about an incident that happened in my life way back in the way back when—an occurrence I haven't thought about in years...

I was sitting in the apartment of, *"My girlfriend."* I put girlfriend in quotations marks as we were like twelve years old and you know how it is when you, *"Liked,"* somebody back then. Anyway, the way her apartment was set up, somebody could knock at the rear door and you could only see the one person standing directly in front of the glass window on the door. The person knocking was the guy I considered my best friend. He waved for me to come out. I opened the door, walked outside, and immediately got jacked by his brother and three or four other guys. The moment I stepped out BAM, I got punched in the side of my face. These kids were maybe four years older than me so they had a lot more weight and savvy than I did—four years makes a lot of difference at that age. One of the guys was one of those big burly

14

Mexicans who had been held back a few grades so he was even bigger. And, the punches continued. All I could do was to keep fighting back and that is what I suggest to everyone, no matter how many people are attacking you, you gotta keep punchin' no matter what!

From a technical perspective one of the things attacking gangs do not realize is that it is hard for several people to all punch at a person at once. I had already been training in the fighting arts for several years and I used that knowledge to my advantage. But, the fact is, in those situations, you are going to get hit and, at best, you can just try to keep swinging back. Forget about what you see in the movies 'cus that ain't gonna happen.

In the midst of all that, I remember looking to my supposed, *"Best friend,"* as he stood over to the side watching what was going on. He did nothing. Finally, with me refusing to submit and my, *"Girlfriend,"* screaming, the attack was over and I was promised it would recommence sometime later. I walk away a bit bruised but not too much worse for the wear.

Later, I asked my supposed best friend why did he do that? His answer, *"He's my brother."*

Being an only child and having a virtually non-existent extended family I realized that I never even thought about something like that. …How a person would choose a family member over a friend simply because they were a family member. But, that is life. That is reality. Just look at your family structure. For all of you who have brothers and sisters and cousins; sure you may get into beefs with them but at the end of the day they are most often forgiven, as they are your family. For the most part, no matter what definition you place on your friends, they are going to come and go, and if a choice has to be made between you (a friend) and family, you will not be the one chosen.

So, what does this tell us about life? First of all, life is a violent place. It shouldn't be, but it is. Whether this violence is enacted by physicality, verbal assaults, or simply by the directed or uncaring actions of others; you most likely, at some point, will be attacked. It's not right. But, it is the way it is. This is especially the case when someone comes at you with a bevy of people to support their attack.

From an intellectual perspective we can all say, *"That's wrong."* But, look to your own life, who have you attacked, who have you hurt, who have you done damage to through your words, deeds, or punches?

Moreover, whom do you side with in life? And, why do you side with them? Why do you choose a side at all? Why? Because you choose to have a perspective. Because you choose to have an opinion. Because you want to be right. But, is your right the ultimate right? Or, is your right simply your perspective or they way in which you want other people to behave?

In life there will be confrontation(s). For those of us who base our lives upon consciousness, we always try to accept and understand another person's perspective—we don't want to hurt anyone. But, not all people are like that. Some people want to use force to get people to behave the way they want them to behave; say and do what they want them to say and do. So, when you are attacked what can you do? If you don't want to die all you can do is to keep punchin'.

If you are planning an attack, don't do it, because that is just the wrong way to behave and interact with other people. And, if you care about a person, if you care about people, if you understand that you are not the only person who is right, then there is no need for an attack at all.

The Processing of Anger
12/Aug/2018 08:08 AM

Have you ever encountered a situation where you found yourself becoming angry but instead of allowing that emotion to take control over you, instead you decided to not become angry? As anger is an emotion that means that you have the ability to control that emotion. You possess the ability to not let it control you. Yes, most people do not choose to develop the ability to take control of the switch that turns anger on and off in their psyche but that control is possible for those who choose to exercise that control.

Anger is a learned emotion. Anger is a developed emotion. Anger is a controlling emotion. But, as it is learned, developed, and controlling, it too can be taken control over.

People learn how to express anger early in their life. They initially learn how to express anger from their parents and family. This is why if a person is born into an anger-driven, abusive family they are more than likely to have little control over the emotion of anger and thereby spread that emotion onto all they encounter. This is why the abused oftentimes become the abuser.

In some cases, people with brain injuries, psychological deformities, and biological mental defects like the varying and sometimes undiagnosed forms autism do not possess a sense of control over their anger. Something has gone haywire in their brain and they lack control over the processing center that most people possess. From this, and other reasons, anger is allowed to breed within and from these people.

At the center of the emotion of anger is a person choosing to be angry. Just like a child who throws a tantrum and from that unacceptable behavior is finally given what they want, a person who uses anger is doing so to get something that they desire. In some cases, they may not even know what they actually want. But, none-the-less, they use anger to gain that abstract something.

Think about your own life. Think about the times you have become angry. Has that expression of anger gotten you what you wanted? Did it get another person to behave they way you wanted them to behave? Or, did it simply create a person who was angry at you for you being angry and a person who now distrusts you because you were behaving in a negative, uncontrolled manner?

Anger is a learned emotion. Anger is a developed emotion. Anger is a contagious emotion. Anger is intergraded into a person's mental vocabulary by choice. As anger was introduced to you, you can choose to control how you behave when you experience this emotion. Learning to take control over the emotion of anger is one of the highest states of human consciousness because anger is one of the lowest expressions of human consciousness.

Be more than your anger. Do not let it control you. For, with one person control their anger, their anger does not spread onto others and the everything of the world becomes just a little bit better.

It seem that we frequently hear about the sexual adoration of spiritual teachers in the news all the time. If we look into any spiritual teaching it becomes quite clear that there is a never-ending tale of sexual and power-driven impropriety being unleashed on the congregates. And, this has been going on throughout time. As we've moved into the modern era, it appears that these stories have come to be more spoken about. But, if they are happening now, they were surely happening way back, in the way back when, where the voices of people were far more held to silence. But, the question must be asked, how and why is spirituality a source point for aberrant sexual and physical behavior? The answer, in brief; power.

For everyone who is drawn to living a life based upon spirituality somewhere deep inside themselves arises the understanding that there is something greater out there than simply living a day-to-day existence. Whether the person seeks to simply be a good example to others while following their spiritual teaching or if they want to be a vehicle for their god and/or find enlightenment, they internally understand that to do so they must embrace a different pathway than the everyday experience of the everyday person.

Due to any number of reasons there are some people who decide that it is their calling to become a spiritual teacher and guide others down the pathway towards god realization. Certainly, in and of itself, this is not a bad thing. Most of these people, I would imagine, never enter this pathway believing it will be a means for them to control others and to take advantage of the diminished position of the people of their order. Yet, with position comes authority and with authority comes ego. From ego is born all of the dastardly deeds done to society.

Not all people who rise to a position of spiritual authority choose to do so. Throughout history there have been those people who spiritual authority has simply been cast onto them. In this modern era there have been great sages like J. Krishnamurti who was positioned to be the next messiah. A position that he rebuked. The current, fourteenth, Dalai Lama was placed in his position as a young child. He has followed through teaching his tradition and bridging cultural gaps throughout his lifetimes. Though any teacher is sure to have a sense of ego in what they are doing, there have been those, like the aforementioned individuals, who have chosen to not let this ego dominate their mission. On the other hand, there are those who have reveled in their power.

I could give a long list of names of spiritual teachers who have been accused and in some cases convicted of using their power to dominate the minds and bodies of the constituents. Whether or not they were consciously aware of what they were doing or were simply driven by an inner demon almost does not matter. What they did damaged the life of the seeker, and in some cases took the life of the seeker, and this is the ultimate sin for the religious.

This brings us to why do people do this and how do they get away with doing it? Think about yourself, do you desire spiritual knowledge? Now, I realize, many people out there who read this blog do not. And, that's fine. That is just who you are. But, for those of you who do have a mind tilted towards spiritual realization, where have you found your knowledge, who have you turned to in order to be taught? No doubt, a teacher. Thus, by the very path to advancing human knowledge that you choose to walk, you are the one who has put the power into the hands of these people.

Certainly, when you have turned to a minister, a priest, a rabbi, a murshid, a guru, or a whatever, you have not gone to that person expecting to be abused. Yet, with each person who turns to them, the interpersonal knowledge of their power grows and if they have the mind for it, they may shift to believing that they have archived something worthy of worship or at least something that allows them to use their position to gain any desire they hold. Thus, each person who turns to a teacher is responsible for a providing them with the power to use and damage the life of other people.

A simple equation to calculate is how much money are you asked to give to your church? Which, in essence, is money given to the primary teacher of that church. You are paying their salary. Thus, you are proving them with a vehicle to commit their sins.

Now, many people believe that this is way it is supposed to be, to give money to their church. But, is it the way it is supposed to be if this person abuses their power? And, by providing sustenance to a person in this position of power you are continuing the tradition that even if your own teacher does not personally exploit his or her power another person down the road may.

So, the spiritual aspirant is the one who is actually providing the means for abuse within all spiritual traditions to take place. This is a sad truth but it is the truth.

Though there is no ultimate answer for this quandary. None-the-less, this is what you must contemplate when you turn to any teacher, teaching any tradition of spirituality. If you provide them with the power, that power may take control over their mind causing them to do bad things. And, though they may not personally embrace this aberrant lifestyle one of their students, somewhere down the road may. Thus, knowledge gives birth to power, power gives birth to ego, ego gives birth to domination, domination gives birth to damage.

Self knowledge is the ultimate knowledge.

You may want something to be what you want that
something to be but just because you want it to be
that way does not make it so.

09/Aug/2018 02:05 PM

You can look for an answer in the same place forever but if the answer does not exist you will never find it.

09/Aug/2018 07:50 AM

You can't coast when you're driving uphill.

Experience is Everywhere.
Enlightenment is Everywhere.
08/Aug/2018 06:17 AM

People believe that they must travel somewhere to gain something. They think that if the go out there, (to that place), they will then find what they are looking for. The problem with this ideology is, however, out there is always out there and with it being the out there, there can never be any control over what you will encounter. Yes, you may want to find something. Yes, you may have heard that it can be obtained out there but as you have no control over the out there, what you will actually encounter is a hoped for promise at best.

People travel to Hollywood to become a movie star. People travel to India to find enlightenment. But, out there is not a finite place. Out there is a million minds each operating from a perspective of their own desire. From this, they never open a door for anyone to enter unless it serves their own particular purpose. Thus, whatever desire, whatever you hope you hope to find out there is dominated by the desire-filled minds of everyone who is already there.

When someone obtains the obtainment they desire, that obtainment becomes a personally relished treasure. Few are willing to share it. From this is born the hierarchy of Hollywood and the, *"Hidden Secret Truth,"* of enlightenment.

Nobody wants to tell you what he or she knows. No one wants to share what he or she has obtained. Thus, all that arises is the promise of and the never-ending verbal mumbo-jumbo that places a barrier between what you want to achieve and what you are allowed to achieve. From this, most people become more damaged from walking the trail to their desired end-goal than those who truly find fulfillment in the process.

Have you ever noticed in your life that sometimes you find the greatest happiness in your own home? Have you ever realized that sometimes you find the greatest gratification in some local location that you never even thought about as a place of fulfillment? Have you ever observed that sometimes the greatest sense of accomplishment is achieved by doing something small and controlled within your own control?

You don't have to go to Hollywood to become a star. You don't have to go to India to find nirvana. All you have to do is to accept the perfection of the reality that you find yourself defined within. For within that perfection is not only self-defined control of your reality but safety for yourself, as well—as you are not looking to anyone else to find what you are seeking.

If you don't have to look outside of yourself to find what you believe you are looking for, you are free. In freedom arises the everything. It is in freedom that you allow yourself to achieve without artificially attaining. It is being enlightenment, within the absolution of enlightenment, that you will find the need of no-need to be schooled in the pathway to enlightenment. For it is in this space of mind that you allow you to realize the ultimate truly of reality—enlightenment is everywhere. For anyone who as arrived at the end-goal of enlightenment understands, we all already are enlightened, we simply have to embrace this fact.

So, instead of desiring to travel out there to get what you want, be who you are in your own field of perfection and let what you are surrounded with be your all and your everything—let it become what you need to gain what you want.

*　　*　　*

08/Aug/2018 06:15 AM

How much are you thinking about what that other person needs right now?

*   *   *

08/Aug/2018 06:13 AM

If you can't face studying yourself in the mirror, you will never know what you truly look like.

31

*   *   *

Ask yourself, *"What can I do today to make someone else's life better?"*

Are you willing to do it?

Fighting the Marketplace
06/Aug/2018 09:44 AM

There is a certain group of people who, for whatever reason, truly wish to succeed in life. There are also others, who wish to do nothing with their life. Which personality is better? I guess there is no absolute answer for that question but what occurs from these differing mindsets are two distinct life-paths. One of them is focused and desire-driven; leading to living a life that is rarely fulfilled. The other is a life lived in the peripheries: silent and content.

For the person who is driven to succeed, they do many things to achieve that success. In fact, many will do whatever it takes. But, what does it take to succeed? That definition is different in each case but the one thing that is certain is that the person with their eyes set on success rarely takes into consideration the impact they are having on anyone else. All they see is the end-goal and everyone else in the world be damned.

As a person who has been involved in (at least) two professions that are defined by success-driven people, I have watched as many a person has passed through their life defined by their desire. I have also witnessed many a person doing whatever they believed it took to achieve their desire while not only damaging their own life and karma but the lives of many other people.

Let's look at these two aforementioned professions...

I have been making movies for over thirty years. I have met so many would-be grand filmmakers and will-be movie stars that I cannot even come close to giving you the number. They all say the same thing by varying words, *"I was destine to do this." "This is my true passion." "This is my calling." "I will be the one who makes it."* I meet them, maybe I am able to help them a bit and give them a crew position or a role and then what? They are gone, never heard from again.

But, more than that, though I may have interacted with them for a moment or two, what else happened with their lives by the choices they made? What impact did they have on others: their family and friends? I have witnessed so many people throw their lives away based on nothing but this desire to succeed; doing horrendous things. I have watched how they have hurt their own life, done bad things for bad people—causing them to lie, cheat, and hurt other people; their family and friends. We've all heard the stories. It is just that I have witnessed some of them. But, what was the end result? Not only did the person who had enacted the desire get hurt but the lives of all of the people in their wake were also damaged. But, to what end? The person did not become a grand filmmaker. The person did not become a star. So, what did it all mean?

The other profession that I can reference with a lot of personal experience is that of running a martial art business. I have been involved with the martial arts for most of my life, well over fifty years.

Over the years I've written a lot about the modern martial art mindset and how, sadly, many a modern practitioner bases their entire personal reality upon attacking and demeaning other martial artists. I believe this is based upon personal insecurity but I guess why a person chooses to do what they choose to do can only be ultimately defined by the individual. Whatever the case, a person sets up a studio and goes to work trying to keep student under their roof. But, at what cost?

By their very nature, the martial arts are a good thing. They not only teach a person self-defense and self-confidence but how to find a deeper understanding of body and mind control. But again, I cannot even tell you how many professional martial artists I have met that base their entire reality upon attacking others. *"That guy is no good. I'm better." "That school teaches crap martial arts. My school teaches the best."*

As a sub-profession, I am a journalist. That was never by choice, it was just something that came after me. But, for a number of years I worked for this one magazine where pretty much on a monthly basis I was asked to interview a martial arts professional about various training and marketing methods for school owners. I cannot tell you how many lies I was told about how great their school was, how they had thousands of students and were making millions of dollars, how their training and marketing method was the best, and how everyone should join their organization. But, where are all these school owner's now? Gone, in the wind…

As a person who operated a martial art school myself, from the late 1970s into the 1980s, I can say from experience it is no way to make a secured living. But, I did it for fun and for the purpose of karma yoga. I never care about the money. In fact, I taught for free for years.

But, there is it, the martial arts… A person desires, focuses, trains hard, and dreams of becoming a black belt. They earn one and then what? To own a school, they end up needing to speak ill of other school owners to maintain a student body. Not good… And, as I always say, if anyone says anything judgmental or bad about any person that should be your warning to steer clear of that person.

These are just two examples. But, the world of cutthroat-desire spans all walks of life. Look at all the bullshit that goes on in the corporate world, the sales world, the banking world, the world of finance, and the government; forget about it…

So, what does this tell us? What does this tell the person who has a desire to become?

The answer: it lets us know that at they heart of living a good life is to pursue what you desire to pursue, as that is a condition of life, but you must do it with goodness as your central beacon of definition. You must never rise by causing another person to fall. And, you must realize that whenever you desire to become anything, the overwhelming fact is that you will probably not success. Why? Because reality is not solely based upon what you desire. Reality is a conglomeration of what everyone else desires. So, be prepared to fail. Thus, never do anything that will hurt your overall life definition. Never do things that hurt anyone else's overall life definition. For if you hurt anyone, yourself included, all you will be left with is the karma and the destiny of hiding from and lying

36

about what you have done or regretting what you did not become.

06/Aug/2018 08:20 AM

Do you think about what you do before you do it?

Do you think about why you are going to do something before you do it?

Do you contemplate who will be affected by what you do before you do it?

Do you care about any of these questions?

*   *   *

06/Aug/2018 07:23 AM

How content can you be with where you find yourself in life?

*   *   *

06/Aug/2018 07:22 AM

If you refer to God as Joe and every time you hear the name Joe you think of God, what's the difference?

What Do You Think About When You Wake Up?
05/Aug/2018 08:01 AM

When you wake up in the morning what is the first thing that you think about? For most, it is perhaps analyzing the dream they just had, anticipation or trepidation about the day that they are about to live, whom they love or whom they hate, maybe that they must quickly get up and feed the kids, or maybe they lay there and fantasize about the person they want to be with or the life they wish to live. What virtually no one wakes up and contemplates is how to focus their mind and live a more focused, spiritual, and consciously refined existence.

On the *Spiritual Path,* one of the key components is to rise from the sleeping state and formally enter into interacting with the cosmic mind. It is for this reason that it is taught that you must train your body and your mind to rise at a specific time each day, formally prepare, and then sit for meditation. With this, the faulty and flawed definitions of the ego and the human mind are replaced with an understanding of cosmic awareness. But, who does this? Virtually nobody.

Think about your life. Think about the things you are doing with your life. Why are you doing them? There is no right or wrong answer for this, just think about it… Why are you doing what you are doing?

For most, their life is filled with a never-ending list of uncontrolled emotions and unfulfilled desires. They feel what they feel, they want what

41

they want. But, they do this with absolutely no mental control. This is the birthplace of karma for from this mindset a person wants to achieve what they want to achieve, they want to feel what they want to feel, and to actualize these goals they do not think about who or what they are hurting in the process. As they possess no sense of refined consciousness, as they do not contemplate the greater mind-space of cosmic awareness and enlightenment, all they are focused on is Self and what that Self wants. Even if they think about their Self giving something to someone else, that is still them, personally, giving something to someone else. Thus, that thought is not based in the *Pure Mind*. It is simply another thought dominated by ego.

There are many people who go to their church or their temple on their holy day. They may listen to the words their congregational leader speaks for an hour or so. But then, all that sense of spiritual refinement is gone. That's it for the week. Back to the world of thinking about Self.

So again, what is the first thing that you think about when you wake up in the morning? Do you ever contemplate this? Do you ever contemplate why you think those thoughts?

No matter what religion you practice or what you do or do not believe in, there is one fact that is absolute, if you do not live your life from a place of refined consciousness all you will continue to encounter is happiness and sadness, exhilaration and anger, fulfillment and loss. All you will continue to feel is whatever your uncontrolled thinking mind causes you to feel. And, for most, they never even try to understand why they are feeling what they are feeling. Thus, enter all the complications of interpersonal relationships and the greater troubles of the world as a whole.

So, who do you want to be? Do you want to be the person who is out of control of yourself, dominated by undefined, uncontrolled emotions and by others? Or, do you want to be the best person you can be: whole, complete, with a sense of refined internal knowledge?

If you want to the ladder, it takes time. It takes control. It takes refinement.

When you wake up in the morning what do your think about? Instead of letting your unfettered mind decide where your thoughts will run, why don't you take control, consciously turn off for a few moments, and meditate.

*　　*　　*

04/Aug/2018 10:41 AM

If you want someone to pay you for just being you,
<u>you</u> better have a lot to offer.

*　　*　　*

04/Aug/2018 10:40 AM

There's a reason for everything. But sometimes people aren't honest about what that reason is.

*   *   *

04/Aug/2018 07:54 AM

In the world of doing, what are you doing?

Do you ever question yourself while you are doing?
Do you ever ask, *"Don't I have anything better that
I should be doing?"*

If you live your life based upon desire two things occur:

One: When you are young you work towards achieving your desire believing that someday it will materialize.

Two: When you are old you regret not have achieved what you desired.

Remove desire from the equation and what are you left with? The answer, freedom, perspective, understanding, and a life not having been defined by striving for the unobtainable.

Active Verses Reactive Consciousness
02/Aug/2018 09:03 AM

How much time do you spend contemplating what you are going to do? How much time do you spend happy, sad, elated, or angry over something someone else said or did? How much control do you possess over what you will do next in your life?

All life is defined by the realities of where we find our self in life. All life is then defined by how we choose to act and react based upon where we find our self in life. All life is actualized by what you think in your mind, causing you to do what you do and react the way you react. How much control do you possess?

For most, they never even contemplate the idea of self-definition and self-control; they simply do, defined by external realities. Life has placed them there, thus they do that. Someone said this, thus they say that. But, this is not consciousness. This is simply giving into the reactive mind. Meaning, a person who behaves in this manner has no self-definition, self-determination, or self-control. Thus, they are not themselves; they are simply what the world has created.

Who are you? Are you what the world has created or are you what you have created?

Why do you think what you think? Why do you do what you do? If you are not in constant possession of the defining factors to those questions then you are living a life not defined by yourself, you are simply living a life defined by the everything else.

Many people, when presented with these questions, immediately go to cultural or psychological rationalizes. I am this way because...

But, this is not self-knowledge, this is simply self-denial. It is removing your responsibly for the person you are, the person you have become, and the person you will become. Thus, there is no sense of true internal understating when someone dismisses a question about Self with an answer like that.

Admittedly, most people do not care about why they are what they are, why they do what they do, and what affect it has on the greater whole of the world. As long as they are well fed and relatively happy they never ponder anything. This is the same with a person who bases their life upon dissatisfaction. They are unhappy, thus they look for a reason to project that unhappiness onto the world. ...End of story and end of self-investigation.

A true life, a truly good life, is based upon the actions you take emanating consciously from your own focused inner being. But, to get that that stage of human evolution takes single-minded work. You are not going to arrive there simply by being who you already are and behaving in any manner that suits the emotions that you are feeling in any given moment. Enter, focused self-investigation.

To know yourself, to understand yourself, you initially need to investigate yourself. This is a complicated process because the thinking mind is full of all kinds excuses it presents to you providing you with a formula for you dancing around the truth of who and what you truly are.

We all wish to be something. But, is that something who we truly can be or do we simply pretend that we are something that we are not? Without deep self-investigation we can never reach the reality of our true reality and come to an actualized understanding of who and what we truly are and who and what we can actually become.

Your life is not simply what you want your life to be. Your life is defined by all of the factors that makes the true and internal you who that person actually is. If you cannot move past the delusion of what society, family, and your own deluded mind has projected onto you, you can never be who and what you truly, actually are. This is why there is so much chaos, based upon the mind applications of what people personally set in motion in this world. What they are doing is not what they should be doing but simply a projection of their ego and their exaggerated sense of self. Thus, is born a world where there is more fantasy than reality, more destruction than elemental creation.

Each person's life is a gift. Each person's life is defined by what they present to the world. Without a refined sense of interpersonal deep understanding no one can be their true self leading to the greater good. Instead, all they can be is a projection of their ego, which leads to never-ending karmic reactions.

Take the time and care enough to know yourself. Find out who and what you truly are, why you do what you do, and why you react the way you react. With this knowledge in place formalized self-control is no longer necessary because you will be living in a space of perfected reality where all you do is provide a pure service based upon refined inner-knowledge to the world. Thus, you help and never hurt; you give but never take.

*   *   *

There is who you claim to be and then there is who you truly are.

Which one do you project to the world?

*   *   *

01/Aug/2018 02:25 PM

What do you buy when you can't afford what you want?

*　　*　　*

01/Aug/2018 08:14 AM

What decision do you make when there's no good decision to be made?

Why Am I Not Allowed To Have An Opinion?
01/Aug/2018 07:49 AM

The moment you enter the public eye everything in your life changes. It seems that no one wants you to have an opinion. Or, perhaps better stated, they only want you to have an opinion they agree with. If you don't, they set about on a course to trash your name by any means possible. I mean, all you have to do is to look around at this moment in history and listen to the news and there are accusations and false claims flying everywhere. But, the thing about accusations are, they are not necessarily the truth, they are only the way one person wants the truth to be perceived and, thus, they use media and social media to make a person appear bad whether they are actually bad or not.

I've spoken about this in the past, so I am not going to really do that here but the fact of the matter is, most people believe anything that they hear and they never take the time to seek out the actual truth. Thus, entire lives are ruined simply by someone making a factually inaccurate statement motivated by who knows what?

Ask yourself, do you immediately believe everything that you hear about everybody? Do you actually believe something about someone else simply because someone said it? If you do, you really should rethink your educational model.

For me, I have witnessed this mindset forever and it always perplexes me. Why is someone like me not allowed to hold an opinion and if I do, it becomes a reason for attack. For example, if I don't like a business or get screwed over and mention it on Yelp, it pisses people off and they attack. They don't care about what I went through. They just want a reason for attack. And, that is just one example.

It is the same with physical conflict. People question why do I always speak so vehemently against fighting. Certainly, physical combat is the lowest level of human evolution but that is not really the point. I have told this story (better) somewhere else, sometime, along time ago, but maybe twenty years ago or so the reality of Scott Shaw fighting was clearly brought into focus for me. There was this guy breaking hard and trying to start a fight with me but he hedged his bet, before any confrontation could actually take place he so poetically stated, *"You will probably kick my ass but then I am going to call the police and have you arrested for assault and then I am going to sue you."* I mean, there I was, a person who had written tons and tons of stuff on the martial arts and was very well known as a martial artist, so who were the people going to believe? At least it caused me to have a reason to walk away.

I mean, even with *Zen Filmmaking,* a system I very consciously put together to actually help the indie filmmaker get their films made. But, I have received tons of attacks based upon that concept. But, are the attackers actual filmmakers? Have they ever made a film? Have they ever actually made a film *Zen Filmmaking Style?* For if they had, I believe they would have realized the help it provides because everyone I have heard from who has used the system has liked it. Moreover, have they actually read what I have written about filmmaking? For what I say is the lived-truth and my words are designed to provide help and remove common obstacles. Have those critics actually lived a life in the film industry? Have they ever received actual distribution for a film they made? Are they here in Hollywood and are they actually active in the business? If not, they do not and cannot understand the reality and the complexities of the film industry that exists nowhere else in the world. They may not like what I say, they may have heard I said something I didn't say, they may not like the films I create but they have no valid reason for attack because they do not and cannot understand the reality of the independent film industry. None-the-less, they want a reason to attack so they focus on me in association with *Zen Filmmaking*. But, those attacks are not based in the reality of actually knowing, they are simply based in a person looking for a reason to attack.

These are just a couple of example based upon the perspective of me. I am sure you each have your own stories to tell.

The thing I believe that this teaches us is that most people never take the time to truly know what another person is thinking or why they say what they say or do what they do. Thus, you should not look for a means for attack for, if you do, that only proves that you are a person who attacks for the sake of attacking which makes you an uncaring, unstudied, unactualized individual. And, that is not a good thing.

People are who they are, no matter what their placement in society. They think what they think and they do the best that they can in life.

Some people, like myself, may be a bit more prolific with what they create, write, or say but you don't see me attacking people. I respect everyone even if don't like what they're saying or doing.

So, think about this before you set up your next smear campaign or fall into one that someone else has instigated. Respect all life. Respect all people. Honor their opinion. And, let them be who they want to be. Would this not make all life just a little bit better?

The People Who Think They Have
Something to Say
31/Jul/2018 08:17 AM

Have you ever been in one of those situations where you are in an enclosed space and there is someone talking so loud that you are forced to listen every word that they say? Pretty terrible; right? And, why do they do that?

I was having breakfast in this restaurant yesterday and there was this lady sitting with two other people and she was talking so loud, it was almost like she was giving a lecture to the whole restaurant. She talked and talked, completely ruining the environment and the gastronomic enjoyment for everyone. Ever now and then she would ask one of the other two people a question. They would give a rudimentary answer and then she would chime in, over-talking them, and go right back into her discourse. It was terrible. It really ruined my breakfast and I imagine it ruined the breakfast of a lot of other people.

I have taught a lot of classes in my life— more than I can even remember. Whether it was teaching the martial arts, seminars, or courses at the college or university level, I understand that projection of the voice is important in those situations. But, a person who does not have control does not have control and at best they are simply locked into a egotistical mindset that they feel they have something to say that the world should hear. But, the world does not want to hear it!

I think back to this horrible neighbor I once had. The guy moved in and he was so loud, speaking with his windows wide opened, that he ruined everything for all of his neighbors. He fancied himself some sort of spiritual teacher so he would lecture people over the phone and on the internet at maximum volume for hours upon hours. When he was not doing that he was stomping on the floor and screaming, *"Fuck me,"* over and over again. Obviously, he was completely out of self-control but yet he marketed himself as a spiritual teacher. It was really bad, for a couple of years I did not even want to go home because I knew I would have to listen to his bullshit that went on day and night. He rarely left his residence. Eventually, I moved but even today when I bump into one of my old neighbors at the supermarket the first thing she says to me is, *"Do you remember how horrible it was living by that guy?"* So, his loudness really ruined a lot of lives. And, it still, years later, has an affect on those of us who had to live through it. In fact, when I finally confronted the guy about it, did he say, *"Sorry?"* No, he just made up excuses. The guy should be really ashamed of himself but I doubt that he is. And, here lies the ultimate definition of being spiritual, (something he falsely proclaimed to be), if you are truly spiritual, you understand that you make mistakes and once you know that you have made a mistake you do all that you can to repair any damage that you created. He did not. Just like the lady in the restaurant yesterday, he was so self-involved that he was not even self-aware enough to understand or to care about how he was damaging the lives of other people by broadcasting his bullshit that no one wanted to hear, to the world.

So, what does this tell us about people? And, what should we do if we encounter a situation like this?

First of all, never believe that what you think or what you have to say should be broadcast to the masses for that is nothing but egotistical mind fuck bullshit. You do not have a special gift or special knowledge. Secondarily, if you have something say, say it with quiet dignity. If you are in a public place or a space where others may be forced to hear your words, keep the volume of your voice lowered to a controlled, personal level for your words are your words and they should be interactively spoken so only the person you are with may hear them. Finally, if you are in a situation like I found myself yesterday, confrontation only equals further confrontation so going and telling them to, *"Shut up,"* or *"Keep it down,"* will not be heard because the person is lost in their own egotism. The fact is, the person who speaks unnecessarily loudly, is a lost soul based in an egotistical mindset and they are not worth the confrontation.

Welcome to life… Sometimes you have to deal with stuff you just don't want to deal with. As a person of consciousness, the best thing you can do is put in the ear buds and move along to where you find a more peaceful, spiritual, and calm place to exist. This is not necessarily easy but it is the only way to consciously get through life when you encounter those situation or those people that you know you should just not have to deal with.

*   *   *

If you live your life defined by your emotions, you will be forced to live an emotional life.

*   *   *

Most people don't think before they do. That is why they do what they do.

Most of the world's problems are born from the unthinking mind.

30/Jul/2018 07:21 AM

If every day is just another day pretty soon all of your days will be gone.

30/Jul/2018 07:20 AM

How much time do you spend being thankful for what you have compared to thinking about what you want?

People, Life, and the World of Whatever
28/Jul/2018 08:02 AM

When the first Starbucks hit the shores of Los Angeles in 1990 and then quickly expanded across the whole city it used to be a place where the young, the cool, the hip, the trendy, and the artsy worked. Whenever and wherever you would go into a Starbucks you would see one of the pretty people. It was kind of an interesting/strange experience that I took note of. As they years have gone along I began to see this change, however. A new breed of person came to work for the company. It became more staffed by the people who just needed a job and couldn't find one elsewhere. In the recent decade or so I have encountered some strange and different people who came to be barista at Starbucks that were definitely not artsy by any stretch of the imagination.

The other day I was in a Starbucks and two of the male employees were talking behind the counter. Instead of discussing the arts, what band they were in, or how they had just auditioned for a play, the one guy was boldly and loudly telling the other barista how a guy had just come in that he had kicked his ass the other day and that he was about to jump over the counter and do it again. *"I hate that piece of shit,"* he loudly exclaimed as customer's heads turned. Wow... Times have certainty changed...

If you ever watch the people who train in jujitsu, particularly Brazilian jujitsu, what you witness is a couple of people rolling around on the ground attempting to get the better of each other.

Though there are certainly rules of combat in these schools of self-defense but to the untrained eye, it ends up just being a sweat fest of two people rolling around on the floor. In fact, sometimes when I teach seminars in traditional schools of martial arts I instruct the students to take each other to the ground and see who will emerge victorious as this style of combat provides a great education in how quickly a person's energy is depleted and how chaotic undefined combat can be.

Certainly, in the more formally defined schools of combat they teach very exacting techniques to countermand the ground fighting assault of an attacker. But, these counter measures are designed to truly damage, (maybe for life) that assailant. In my younger days, whenever I had gotten into a tussle and ended up in a ground fight where many a street fight ends up, I always warned the opponent, *"Let go or I am going to hurt you."* And, I meant it. At least I was nice enough to warn them. But, all you have to do is to end up rolling around on the ground with a fighting opponent to realize the ridiculousness of anger-based combat.

In life, there is a certain breed of person who seeks out combat. This mindset can be based upon all kinds of all kinds of stuff. But, they attack and just like the barista they want to tell the tales of their battles. They want to tell somebody else what they have done and what they will do. But, what does any of that energy equal? And, who knows if any of the words they speak are true? Moreover, who cares? What does two people having a fight actually equal?

Some people attack people. Some people speak of attacking people. Some people say things behind the back of people in hopes of hurting them. Some people instigate confrontation. Some people threaten people. But, until you are rolling around on the ground you cannot realize the futility of combat. Maybe one person will win. Maybe no one will win. But, all that this aggressive mindset does is to negatively enforce all of the bad things of this world. It does no-thing for no-one.

So, what does this tell us about life? It tells us that people who throw around strong words, the people who focus on confrontation, the people who instigate confrontation are the people who are lost in their own projected image of self and should not be listened to. They are the ones who are making things worse, never better. For, at the end of the day, do you really care about who bested whom in a street fight? Or, who a person hates? What do we care about? Most of us care about happiness, the people we love, and the people who make us feel happy. And, all the other stuff is just mind stuff bullshit projected by one negatively based person onto the world of whatever...

I wish Starbucks was still like what it was, way back in the way back when... A place where the cool and the artsy worked. Where you talk about music, art, poetry, and cinema. Not a place where you go and listen to boldly meaningless spoken words of confrontation.

*　　*　　*

27/Jul/2018 11:45 AM

The reason why most people don't succeed is because they are unfocused and lazy.

The reason why the people who do succeed can succeed is because they don't care about the impact they are having on other people.

What You Do And How You React
To What You Have Done
27/Jul/2018 07:58 AM

Your life is lived on two levels. The first is in your mind. Here, your thoughts and your actions can run wild. Based upon dreams and desires there is no factually defined reality. You can think anything you want. In your mind's eye you can do anything you want. This is also here where you concoct what you will do on the second level of your life.

The second level of life is true reality. This is the place where definitions have an actuality. Where you encounter life situations and people and where what you have thought, leading to what you have done, has a consequence.

Think about a time where you did something to someone that affected him or her in a noticeable or substantial way. Maybe they told you that what you did made a difference: either positive or negative in their life, or maybe you could see them react to what you did. First of all, why did you do it? Was it a conscious action on your part? Did you make a plan, set a course, and then take an action? Or, did you simply do some unthinking thing driven by emotions or a lack of pre-thought? In either case, what you did, did something to someone else. Now what? Do you care that what you did affected someone else?

What we do in life—in the reality of reality is what sets the stage for our personal interactions, what we encounter next in life, and how other people define us. Add to this mix that people are going to do things to affect us: both in positive or negative ways and from this other people are going to draw conclusions about us due to what other people have done to us—what they have said about us—leading to how we reacted to an action someone else took.

At the basis of any life action is one person doing one thing to someone else. You did it, now what?

One of the key components in life, taught by all true religions, is compassion. Also emphasized is honesty, and doing on to others as you would hope people would do on to you. In life, in this primary realm of reality, in this place where we all live the majority of our lives—the place where we interact with interactive human consciousness and encounter other people all the time—this is where our life comes to be defined. Though the methods of interaction have changed over history, interaction is one of the primary components of how one is defined in their life. What you do and what you do to others defines the type of person that you are.

So again, let's come back to the primary question, *"What are you doing to other people?"* Think about what you have done. Take a moment and consciously define in your mind something you did that caused a positive response in the life of some person. Next, think about something that you did where you caused a negative reaction. Now, define why did you do it? Was it a consciously thought-out action? Or, was it simply a responsive action directed into reality by something based solely in your own mind?

71

Here is an essential thing to keep in mind, no matter what was the impetus of what you did; you were the one who decided to do it. No matter what or who instigated you to say the words you said or enact the deed, you were the one who did it, leaving you wholly responsible. You did it, now what? How do you feel about what you did and what do you do next based upon what you previously did?

There are basically two levels of reactive response instigated in the mind of a person who has done something. The first is to take joy and find fulfillment in the action—whether that action was positive or negative. This is the lowest level of human consciousness as it is solely based in the personal ego. This is place where karmic reaction is instigated and what causes people to encounter ongoing reactive life interactions.

The second level is that of mindfulness. The action is done, the reaction is studied, and then appropriate secondary life action is taken in order to either solidify the goodness that was activated or to rectify any badness that was enacted.

Where do you find yourself in life? Do you have an active or a reactive mind? Do you only do? Or, once you have done do you care about what you have done?

Think about your own life. Think about when someone has said or done something positive directed your direction. How did that make you feel? Now, flip the coin, think about when someone has said or done something negative directed your direction. How did that make you feel?

Finally, contemplate once that action was done, what further steps did the person take, directed your direction. If what was done was good and positive, what did they do next. If what they did was negative, what did they do next?

Life is all about what you think leading to what you do. A good life is defined by what you have done followed up by what you have done next. When you do something wrong to someone, no matter what the causation factor or your initial motivation, what do you do next? This is the definition of who you are as a person and what will be the ultimate outcome of your life.

Based in the mind side of life, most people never truly study and/or care about what they have done to someone else that has set a course of events into motion in that person's life. At best, they make mind-space excuses. But, think about your own life; think about when someone has done something to you. How did that feel if the person did not care about what they have done?

We all learn in life. We all learn from life. If we are a conscious, thinking, and caring person we know how we should behave and what we should do. How do you encounter life? How do you interact with people: known or not? What do you do once what you have done has been done?

This is your life. You can make it a positive, active experience; helping many but hurting no one. Or, you can live in a space of mind-based judgments and self-projected fantasies leading to deeds where others are hurt by your words and actions and then you do nothing to repair the damage. What do you think is the best life path?

Now that you know, what are you going to do about what you have done?

The Do That You Do
26/Jul/2018 06:06 PM

What do you actually do in comparison to what you want to do? Why do you do it?

What do you actually say in comparison to what you are actually thinking? Why do you say it?

How do you live in comparison to how you would like to live? Why do you live that way?

For most, they will have an answer for each of these questions. The most common answer is that they are defined or trapped by the reality of their life and they must do what they must do to survive. Okay… That's valid. But, beyond that, there is the reality that people want to live—a reality that they never live. They never live it because they do not focus their attention on it and actually do not attempt to live it.

Certainly, ask anyone, and they will tell you that they wish to be a billionaire, a movie star, a sports start, and the like. The fact is, for most, that reality is probably untouchable. Thus, it becomes more of a fantasy than a goal. This being said, what are you doing to do the do that you wish you could do?

In this modern world, things are doable that just a decade ago were untouchable. A person can get their music, their art, their photography, their words, their movies, their comedy seen and heard by million simply by uploading it online. But, do you? Do you take the time to get the you that you want to be out to the masses seen by the masses? Most do not. From this is born anger, frustration, and jealousy; equaling all kinds of additional negative mind stuff, negative emotions, negative words, and negative deeds. But, it does not have to be like that. If you did, then, at least, you would have done. Then all that envy of what others have done will be erased from you. But, do you?

Right now, ask yourself, *"What would you really like to be doing?"* For most, they already have an answer to that question. Why aren't you doing it? Why are you not at least trying to do it?

From a personal perspective, I have spent my whole life doing. I never rest. From this, I have created a lot of stuff. Some of this stuff has been more successful, fully actualized, and appreciated than others. From this doing, there have been a few people who question why I do. They may even insult what I do and that I do too much. But, how is that possible? How is doing ever, doing something wrong?

In life, most people appreciate the doing. Everything you like in the out-there is based upon someone doing something. No longer must you be in a specific geographic location to achieve in the doing. You can be anywhere to do anything. You just need to do it.

So, what do you want to do? As long as it is a positive creative activity, as long as it is you creating a creation that is uniquely yours, get out there and do. For without the doing there is nothing done.

I drive this older car. It's kind of at the stage where it's breaking down a lot. I keep taking it to mechanics and spending a lot of money for it to be fixed. But, they never seem to get it right. Then, as mechanics tend to do, they tell me one lie or another about why they (or another mechanic) didn't fix it the last time and why they want to charge me more money to fix it this time.

Anyway, my car took a powder today. It's doing this thing that when the engine gets hot it doesn't overheat but it loses all power and then the engine shuts down until it cools down. As I have done before, I coasted it into the nearest parking spot intending to let it cool down for fifteen or twenty minutes.

Where I had broken down was across the street from this small older apartment building. I noticed it while sitting in the heat wave sun that is currently overtaking L.A. but didn't really think that much about it. As I was sitting there, with the sun beating down onto my car, a young lady exited the upstairs apartment and was carrying this large, very beautiful, German Shepard down the stairs. I could see that his (or her) rear legs did not work.

It was obviously a struggle for the young lady as the dog was not light. But, she set him (or her) down in the grass in the front yard of the apartment building. There, the dog began to paw at the grass as if it was trying to walk. Fuck… The whole scene was really emotional. I sat there, in the hot sun and heat of the car, and realized I was crying.

I mean, there she was, this young woman who loved her dog. There he (or she) was, this dog that his or her rear legs no longer functioned. The dog wanted to get up and move but could not. The woman sat there loving and petting the dog. The tears streamed down my face. I hoped she would not notice me.

For anyone who has ever loved an animal, I think you can understand. Pets are, in many ways, more than human because they love you unconditionally. They are the perfect mate.

When I was a young child I had this dog that I totally loved. As I was a latchkey kid, that dog was my best friend. We stayed home alone all day together, while my parents went to work. The dog did not live very long, however. Maybe only two years. It got sick and had to be put to sleep due to contracting Korean Distemper. I guess the name of that disease was a forewarning of what was to become an essential definition of my life. In any case, I was devastated. I remember praying to god every night to please let me have another dog. What I really wanted was to have my dog back but I knew that couldn't happen. I mean, I was all alone. A six year old kid left home alone everyday. But, to this day, I have never gotten another dog. So much for the power of prayer…

I did have this girlfriend once that had a dog that I totally loved. His name was Pablo. We would go for runs around the block where she lived. I think he loved me too. But, you know how it goes;

boyfriends and girlfriends and all… Sometimes things just don't work out.

As I moved into my later adult life, I have had a few Persian Cats. Each one of them has been a unique entity onto itself. And, I have loved them all. When one of them has died it has been devastating. Much more so than when people in my life have passed away. So, what that young lady was doing today, I totally get it. I have no idea what caused that dog to arrive in that the condition that it has encountered and though the situation is very sad, there was the girl, who loved the dog so much that she carried it downstairs, probably every day, and does all she can to give that dog the best life it can live defined by its current condition. What a great thing! What a great love!

I don't know… I wish we all cared about other people the way some people care about their pets. Don't you think the world would be a better place?

Anyway, the dog lay on the grass in the sun, the woman began to water some of the plants in the front yard of the apartment building. Me, I tried my car and it started. I drove off. But, even as I write about this situation, it still makes me feel very sad.

As we each understand, regret is the emotion of deciding or realizing that we should not have done something after we have already chosen to do it. Though the majority of us experience this emotion from time to time, refining our understanding of life and our own psyche to come to a clear understanding of why we make the choices we make, leading to the emotions we feel, and how the choices we make affect other people, is an essential element in coming to embrace the higher version of ourselves.

Think about a time that you felt the emotion of regret. What created that emotion in yourself?

There are a few life actions that commonly are known to cause people to feel regret. One is the common factor known as, *"Buyer's Remorse."* You have purchased something that you wanted and the moment you bought it you immediately realized that it cost way too much and you should not have purchased it. Then, there is, of course, sexual remorse. Driven by desire, you decided or agreed to have sexual relations with a person and afterwards you regretted that choice due to realizing that the person was not who you thought they were or because of all of the social stigma attached to having too many sexual partners.

Though the spending of money and the engaging in sex are too very obvious factors that create the emotion of regret, there are regret creating factors that span throughout the life of each person. But, here is the kicker... Think about the times that you have experienced the emotion of regret. How much of the regret you have felt is solely focused on yourself and how much of the regret you felt is focused on what you have done to someone else?

As people are commonly a selfish creature, for most, all they think about is themselves—all of their emotions are self involved. Thus, what they think about and are focused upon is themselves. Rarely, do people turn their attention, and their regret towards what they have done to others.

Think back to two of the primary factors for creating regret: buying and sex. Does the businessperson who sold you something care about your buyer's remorse? Does the salesperson that talked you into buying something care about your remorse? No, because they are making money. In terms of sex, it is commonly the female who feels the regret after the act, whereas the male feels as if he has made a conquest. Does the male understand the females regret and does he feel sorry for his desire that led to the act being instigated in the first place, which made the female experience the emotion of regret? Probably not.

Here, we are provided with a clear window into the foundations for regret. It is something that one person is feeling and what they are feeling is commonly focused on themselves. They never take into consideration what the someone else is feeling or what they created to make them feel that way.

Take a moment and think about a time that you hurt someone or did something that damaged a person's life—something that made them feel regret. After you did it, maybe you felt good about yourself that you accomplished something. Maybe it made you feel invigorated, maybe it made you money, maybe you added one more trophy to your wall. But, once it was expressed to you or you realized that you hurt someone, in the process of achieving what you viewed as an accomplishment, did it change your emotion about the deed? Did it make you rethink what you had done? Did it cause you to care about what you had put the other person through? Did you care that you hurt them or was that what you were trying to do? Did it cause you to try to erase and/or repair any damage that you created? Or, like most people, did you simply not take the other person's feelings into account, did you make excuses for your actions, and/or did you continue to feel pride in what you had done? If that is how you reacted, what does that say about you as a human being?

All anyone has to do is to remember a time when they felt the emotion of regret to begin to comprehend what is making someone else feel regret. All anyone has to do is to turn their self-thinking mind off long enough and embrace what is going through another person's mind to understand why that person is feeling regret. All anyone has to do is to care enough to think about how what they are about to do is going to affect the person they are about to do it to and then the sociopathic mindset of instigating a situation that will create the emotion of regret in another person will be held in check.

Do you really feel better for doing the things that you believe are accomplishments when they were achieved by instigating regret in the mind of another person?

In life, you have a chance to help people. In life, you have a chance to hurt people. What are you going to do based upon what you desire? Are you going to create hurt and regret or are you going to create joy, hope, contentment, and happiness?

The Guidance You Seek
and Those You Never Thank
24/Jul/2018 08:05 AM

As humans, we all want to do something. In most cases that something we want to do means that we have to learn how to do it. To learn how to do what we want to do we have to turn to someone who knows how to do it. Thus, we need a teacher.

Some people are very good at seeking out a teacher. They are very forceful in their desire and they learn how to do what they want to do and then they do it. Others, not so much. In some cases some people just do not have the force of personality to get out there and learn how to get the job done. Others, though they may take the course, never put what they have learned into action.

All based upon personality, resources: financial and others, and interpersonal drive (which is also a dynamic of personality) people are the force that moves knowledge forward. Some desire to know, they learn, they do, and then they pass their self-developed understanding onto others. This is life.

Though desiring to learn, seeking a teacher, and then learning is one of the formative factors of life, how many people once they have learned something pay tribute to those they have learned it from? For many, there are more reasons to deny any affiliation with a person than to pay them tribute. Why? Because they want to appear to be the source of the knowledge—the beginner of the doing.

Though this style of unthankful behavior is common in life, is it a good thing? Not really. It is more a state of egotism and self-righteousness instead of actualized gratitude.

Think about the people you have learned from. Think about where you would be if you had not come to understand what you have come to understand based upon what they had to teach. Even the people from whom you have learned how not to behave and what not to do—even them, they have taught you something. Think where your life would be if you had never learned anything from anybody.

In life, we all have teachers. In some cases we have sought out those teachers, in other cases they simply came into our life. Whatever the founding factors, we all owe those teachers a lot for without them our knowledge, our understanding, our ability to evolve into our own being would be sharply hindered.

Think about it... What have you learned and whom do you have to thank for acquiring that knowledge? Instead of locking yourself in your own mind. Instead of locking yourself in your own egotism. Why don't you take the time to make a conscious and decided effort to thank the people who have been your teachers—the people you have learned from. You are who you are because of them, appreciate that fact and pay them tribute.

The Idols That You Worship
23/Jul/2018 12:02 AM

In each person's life there is idols that they worship. For some it is religious icons where they are told and they believe that by praying to them they will be speaking with the almighty. For others it is far more temporary things. Maybe it is the hope for a dream job, a dream car, a dream house, or that girl or that guy, off in the distance, that you know if you could only be with them then all of your dreams of love and acceptance would be answered. In other words, people worship all kinds of idols. Most of which they have no ability of ever connecting with. Thus, and because of, this gives birth to all kinds of life-actions that lead to all kinds of life-things all based upon one simple reality, and that reality is, you will never meet the idols that you worship.

Many a religious and self-help figure has spoken about methods to obtain your dreams. They tell you if you believe, if you pray, if your acutely focus your attention upon what you want, you will get what you want all based upon the magical hand of god. They promise you the kingdom but because they do not know you, they do not actually care about you, and they are making money off of you, they will never truly know or understand what you are feeling.

Other people hope to become idols. They place themselves into a prominent position where all the focus is placed upon them. Why do they do this? Whether knowingly or not they do this to draw attention to themselves so that they can draw followers that believe their world and/or develop fantasies about them so that their personal dreams may be fulfilled by the attention, love, energy, and money they receive from others who have focused their mind's upon them.

Look across the globe, how many images of The Buddha or Jesus Christ are there? How many Crosses or Star of David's do people wear around their neck? How many pictures of Gurus and Hindu Gods adorned the walls of people's residencies? A lot.

Why do you think that Islam does not allow people to depict Mohammed in art or images? They do this to keep all of this false idol worship in check.

Most people want something to worship. Why? Because they are not whole in themselves. They want something to dream of achieving. Why? Because they feel unfulfilled. They want someone to fantasy about meeting, falling in love with, and bedding. Why? Because they believe that love will answer all of their needs. But, this mindset is all based upon one simply truth. That truth is, it is not reality. It is something locked into your fantasying mind, placed there by people who have something to gain by you believing in what they have to say.

Think about the people you believe in. Think about the people you listen to. Think about the people you fantasy about. Who are they and why do they do what they do? Do you even know? Do you actually know them? Do you actually know who they are and why they do what they do? Or, are you simply projecting what you believe them to be onto their image? Now ask yourself, how many of the people that you have come to know, that you have come to believe in, that you have come to love are actually what you believed them to be when all they were was a fantasy?

People want to believe. Why do we want to believe? Because each of us has a desire that we want to fulfill.

What is your desire? What has it caused you do? And, whom has it caused you to believe in? If you do not know the answer to these questions you are simply walking through life like most people; desiring but not possessing a clear definition about what you desire and why you desire it.

Define what idols you are worshiping. Find out who they truly are. Why they are someone you find worthy of listening to and/or worshiping. And, what is your idol worship going to cost your life, the life of someone else, and the reality of the greater whole of the world in general. As the age old saying goes, look before you leap. But more than that, know before you leave yourself in a position of unknown tragedy, wreaking havoc onto your own life and the life of others all based upon worshiping false idols.

The Anger Within
21/Jul/2018 08:15 AM

Have you ever had someone that you know: a friend or a family member get mad and go off on you for no reason? You've done nothing wrong—you've said nothing wrong but for some unexplained reason they say some very cruel or untrue thing focused your direction.

Why do people do this? In most cases they are mad at something else or someone else—lost somewhere deep in their own mind. Maybe they are even mad at themselves or the life situation they find themselves unable to control and they are not self-aware enough to understand the inner working of their own mind. Thus, they need a reason to vent and you become the perfect target. Not right but this style of behavior goes on all the time.

Anger is not an unnatural emotion. People become angry all the time. But, it is the person who allows their anger to control them and to motivate them to act in a bad way that sets the stage for bad deeds to be enacted due to their anger.

For many, anger is an undefined emotion. Yes, they know they are angry. Yes, they find a reason to be angry. Yes, they find someone to be angry at. But, few possess the mental maturity to take control over this emotion, follow it to its source, and not let it dominate their behavior.

The people who allow anger to control themselves and their lives are the least mentally evolved human beings. This is why people with the various forms of autism and/or mental illness cannot control their anger as their mind is not fully developed, their sense of defined self is altered and, thus, anger becomes a controlling factor of their psyche.

This being said, there are those people who allow anger to control their actions. With anger as a basis, they say and do bad things and, thereby, create bad feelings from those around themselves and instigate bad deeds that prompt a pattern of distaste and recompense.

Look around, how many people do you know that are angry? Are you angry? All you have to do is to drive down the street in any big city and you will see undefined anger all around you—everyone who freaks out at another driver for a small infraction of motoring protocol, they are a person fueled by undefined anger.

I have always thought that it is very curious to see anger on the internet. Since its inception it has provided people with a vehicle to release that anger and direct it at whomever they wish with little consequence. Thus have arisen the pundits and the trolls of which there is very little difference.

As you watch this anger on the internet you see how people want to attack. But, why do they want to attack? There are obviously a million reasons for this but the fact of the matter is they do want to attack and what is that attack based upon? Anger.

Some people actually possess a self-defined reason to be angry with someone else on the internet. They do not like what that person is saying or what they are doing. One of the things that I have long taken note of, in regard to anger on the internet, is that there is a certain subculture of women who offer various forms of fantasy. Men are a fantasy driven creature so for them, the women who do this provide a great service but they do so at a cost. Maybe one of the most sublets forms of providing this fantasy is the women who appear to be broadcasting from their bedroom. Some do this with a sexual motif. Others simply pretend that this is their only usable studio. In either case, the result is the same. They have given men a reason to dream. From dreams comes hope. From hope comes desire. From desire arises fantasy. But, from unfulfilled desire and fantasy comes anger. Thus, is born a reason to attack, slut shame, and all the rest of those negative anger-based actions. And, this is just one example. Mostly, people with undefined anger simply find something or someone to be angry and focus their attentions in that direction and the internet provides a overabundance of opportunities. But again, this goes back to the sourcepoint of this question, why are they angry? What is missing from their life that causes them to be angry? What are they not receiving and/or what do they not possess that has caused them to allow anger to take control over them?

Do you ever study the actions of a person who is angry at you? Do you ever question why are they angry at you? Do you ever ask them why they are behaving is that manner towards you? This question may be the best question to ask in regard to this subject because most people can only provide a very abstract answer at best. And, this goes to the point of all this. The people who are angry, the people who exhibit anger directed in an undefined manner, the people who do not understand why they are angry and are simply looking for someone to focus their anger upon are the ones who are least in touch with their true inner emotions and unless they are guided towards understanding and coming to terms with these emotions may allow the negative emotion of anger to dominate their entire life. And, this is not a good thing as it hurts people, destroys relationships, and leads a person down a road to doing very bad and very negative things.

So, the moral to this story... If you are angry, figure out why you are angry. If you are behaving in an angry manner towards a person, ask yourself why you are focusing your anger on that person. Make yourself know the answer to these questions. Dig deep and find out who you truly are and what motivates yours emotions. And then, take control over them. For if you cannot do this, all you are is an unrefined slab of clay that no one has taken the time to turn into a beautiful and artistic statuette.

Blind Cruelty
20/Jul/2018 08:17 AM

We live at an interesting juncture of history in that many of the world's peoples live in a space of projected reality. Meaning, they live their lives with their eyes and their mind focused upon their computers and their phones to the degree that they have separated themselves from the truth of true interactive relationships. They simply delve into this world of non-reality and allow their thoughts and their actions to be blindly guided by whatever they see, hear, or read.

Now, the first thing that anyone who follows this life pathway will do is to deny this fact. It is just like if you ever meet a person who smokes and you explain to them that you have known someone who has died from lung cancer, due to smoking, and it is a horrible way to die. They will immediately make up all kinds of excuses for their habit and exclaim, *"My doctor says my lungs are fine," "I don't smoke that much,"* or *"It will not happen to me."* But, it will. ...That or some other cigarette or other smoking substance born disease. Same with motorcyclists. They will negate that they will ever be in an accident. But, they will. It's inevitable. Motorcycling is a dangerous past time.

But, these two examples are based in living a reality. They are based in doing a something. But, the fact is, most people lives have shifted away from the doing and fall simply into the accepting.

For those of you are reading this, most likely you are reading it on your computer, tablet, or your phone. So, here we are... I'm writing this on a computer. You're reading it on a computer, a tablet, or a phone. You're either agreeing with, understanding, and liking what I am saying. Or, it is just the opposite. But, what we are not doing is having a personal, face-to-face discussion. What we are not doing is personally interacting. We are a million miles away from each other, defined by cyberspace. You have your opinion about what I am writing and about me but you have no true bases for that opinion for we never have and probably never will meet. You don't know me. I don't know you. Yet, here we are. Defined by this reality.

Think about it... How many times have you formed an opinion about a person based upon what you have seen, heard, or read on the internet? What are you basing that opinion upon? Is it fact or is it fiction? Is it simply based upon what someone else has said about that person? Or, is based simply upon what you think? In either case, you have never met that person or interacted with them face-to-face so how can you truly know anything about them? For without face-to-face interaction all your reality is based upon speculation. And, this is the point where many of the world's current problems have begun.

As yourself, *"What has what you have believed about a person, that you have never met, caused you to do?"* What have you said about them? Have you hurt someone based upon your beliefs? If you have then you are a part of the problem. For how can you have beliefs about a person if you have not personally interacted with them?

All you have to do is to turn this situation around to gain a deeper understanding. Has anyone

94

you have never met said something about you, causing action to be enacted? If this has occurred then you understand the implications.

In this current definition of reality, life is more interactive than it has ever been. People, even famous people, allow other people to see a projected segment of their lives on places like Twitter, Instagram, and Snapchat. But, is viewing this small portion of their projected reality, knowing them? No, it is not. I remember this person on NPR detailing their story about how they projected to the world that they lived in this great house by only showing photos of a specific portion of it. For on the other side there was this ugly factory that they never photographed. And, this is an ideal example of how people project their personal reality to the world. They only exhibit what they want to be seen. Thus, even if a person is very active online, you can never know who they truly are unless you personally get to know them.

Many people, defined by self-projected exaggerated opinions and by the dissatisfaction they possess with their own life, exhibit a blind cruelty to other people and the world around them. In this world we live in, attacks and the telling of lies and the creation of self-motivated falsehoods is rampant because people never met face-to-face. Yet, people form opinions based upon less than truly defined definitions.

If you have enacted this style of negative behavior, did you ever question, that maybe you are wrong—maybe you are doing something wrong? Maybe what you heard that you have based your opinion upon is false? Maybe if you met the person and came to know them that you may actually like them? Or maybe, if you did meet them they would kick your ass because of what you have said or done based upon your own projection of false reality?

Hurting someone is easy in these modern times. Saying negative things is easy in these modern times. That is the same with helping someone—that is the same with saying something positive. We are all, and we have all always been, defined by where we find ourselves in history. Here we are. This is our point in history. As we are here, what are you going to think, whom are you going to believe, and what are you going to do based upon your belief in a world were virtually no one personally knows anyone yet everyone has an opinion?

20/Jul/2018 08:14 AM

Have you ever given someone some advice and they followed it but then they felt like they made a mistake and they blame you?

What would have happened if you said nothing?

*   *   *
19/Jul/2018 09:03 AM

If you haven't lived what another person has lived
you have no way of understanding their reality.

19/Jul/2018 09:02 AM

The people who cast the most stones are the people who live in a space of denial about their own existence and jealously of the lives of those they cast the stones towards.

*   *   *

19/Jul/2018 09:02 AM

A good lie is always a bad lie.

The Dynamics of Deception

Originally rising out of the Hindu concept of Maya—meaning that all life is an illusion, it is not real; it has long been understood that what we encounter in life is, at best, a projection of our own mental reality. What we see, what we hear, what we speak is entirely defined by the way we personally interpret reality.

As each person passes through life they decide how they define life. Some people are more forcefully judgmental in this actuality than others. They want their reality to be what they want their want reality to be and from this mindset they try to make others believe exactly as they do. Enter religion, politics, psychology, and domination. To achieve this self-defined reality people go to all kinds of length. Some talk, critique, criticize, argue, fight, and create conflict leading to wars. Most, however, project their interpretation of reality by much more subtle methods. They simply lie.

One of the key components about understanding the most elemental factor of truth is that truth, in virtually all cases, is simply an individualized perception. What one person believes to be factual, right, honest, and correct is not what someone else defines using those same parameters. Thus, truth is never an absolute. It is simply a projection of the definition(s) of one person's mind.

With this as a basis, we can each understand that what one person speaks; no matter how emphatically they speak it, what they are saying, is not bound by pure reality it is simply based on what

101

they think. Thus, there is no truth possible when that supposed truth is spoken from the month of one or more people—all there is, is belief. And belief, is at best, wholly defined by the definition of that word. It is one person believing one thing. Thus, it is not truth at all.

This brings us to the so-called projection of truth or one person telling someone else something. When someone speaks do you question, who is saying what and why are they saying it? Do you question, what are they gaining by saying what they are saying? As each person, some more loudly than others, attempts to make people think and believe as they do, these questions must be examined for if you do not analyze each word that you hear—if you simply believe all that you hear—all you have done is to pass the reins of your reality over to someone else and thus you have turned off your own ability to define your own reality. You have simply believed instead of having developed your own truth.

In life, early on some people come to understand that if they are the one speaking, they are the one who is developing believers. Thus, from that following they find internal comfort for whatever they are internally, emotionally, and psychologically lacking. The people who speak the loudest—the people who attempt to pass out the most truth, based on their own interpretation of the truth, are commonly the most internally lacking as they seek followers instead of simply seeking internal knowledge. They seek ego gratification instead of encountering enlightenment. Thus, they are the ones who most emphatically practice the dynamic of deception, as they are the ones attempting to project their interpretation of the truth to the outside world.

As we understand, based upon Hindu and later Buddhist ideology, all life is an illusion. Therefore, instead of attempting to project your interpretation of truth to others, instead of fighting to define a personal truth that may never be truly actualized, instead of attempting to look to others to find that unhaveable truth, be strong enough to put your own ego in check, realize the reality of reality, that your truth is no one else's truth, just as no one else's truth is your truth, and be silent. For only in silence can the ultimate reality of truth, within a realm of no-truth, be comprehended. End deception by only listening to your own inner voice.

Be silent within yourself and the truth of no-truth may be known. With this, deception ends.

18/Jul/2018 08:32 AM

If you don't undo your mistakes your mistakes will never be undone.

What does an ongoing mistake lead to?

18/Jul/2018 08:17 AM

Does saying something negative or judgmental about another person ever make you a better person?

If what you saying, what you are doing does not lead to you become something more, why do it?

*　　*　　*

16/Jul/2018 03:49 PM

One of the most important things to realize in life is that people only describe their own interpretation of the truth.

If you base your life decisions upon what they say you will never find your own truth.

The Sins You Are Given. The Sins You Create.
16/Jul/2018 08:58 AM

We are each born into the world bound by the sins that our parents, our family, and our ancestors have previously committed. Some people are born into a family of vast wealth. How did the previous generation or generations gain that wealth? Some people are born into a family bound by poverty. What personal choices caused the previous generation(s) to be framed by that financial condition? Most find themselves meeting the world somewhere in between; where as a child they have food to eat and a roof over their head but within this realm of seeming safety there are a million other problems that are given birth to from physical and/or emotion abuse, addictions, uncaring, unthinking behavior, onto devastating actions committed by choice. What caused these child bearers to behave in this fashion towards their offspring?

As an infant and a child we are all introduced into a world of sin and karma that we had nothing to do with creating. Though we did not create it, our lives are defined by it. No one can ever completely move to a life realm where they are not defined by the actions of their parents, family, and ancestral predecessors.

The first sin your life will encounter is the sin you were born into defined by your parents and the previous generations of your family lineage. The next sin you will encounter comes at the hands of the chosen actions of your direct family for it is at this level that the sin of choice comes into play.

107

Many people blame many things for the way they behave in their life. Though many of these explanations may sound valid and may, in fact, even be backed up by scientific evidence, there is, none-the-less, one element that comes into play as the primary defining factor for anything any person does and that one defining factor is choice. A person chooses to do something. No matter what the motivating factor for that choice: biological, psychological, or otherwise, someone chooses to do something and from that single choice a plethora of physical and emotional reactions are set into motion that will span throughout the life of the person who made that choice and all of those who were affected by that choice.

Think about how your family treated you as an infant and a child. What specific actions did they take, based upon a choice, that immediately comes to mind? Perhaps these actions were very caring; perhaps they were very cruel and/or hurtful. In either case, view how the choices they made to take those actions came to define you as a person and how you now behave towards other people and how you treat other people based upon those actions of choice.

We are each defined by the sins of our heredity. We are each defined by the way in which our family treated us as a child. We are each also defined by the choices other people made when it came to how they interacted with us. Thus, none of us are whole creations defined solely by ourselves.

As we are not wholly self-defined creatures, what does that tell us about personal choice? Does it tell us that we do have personal choice? Or, does it inform us that we do not—that we are simply a creation of our family, our family environment, and the choices our family and other people made in regard to us?

As we move through life we each make choices that not only affects the next step in our future and our evolution but the next step for all of those who are impacted by that choice. Each choice is a choice that you make. But, each choice possesses the ability to define the entire life of another person. The more interactive your life is with other people, the more choices you make that impact other people. Thus, the more sins you commit. For each word you speak, each action you take, no matter what your motivation is motivated by, that is a choice you have made. Therefore, it is a self-motivated, self-serving choice. And, as we all understand, self-motivation is the basis for sin.

Sin is based in selfishness. Sin is based in desire. As all selfishness, all self-thinking, and all self-thought is the birthplace for what affects the life of not only the instigator but the life of someone else as well; be it good or bad, thus, any action taken is never a pure action as it sets the stage for further sins to be enacted.

What you do affects everyone. It particularly affects those you are close to, those who are forced to abide by your choices, and those who choose to listen to the choices you have made.

You want to know why people suffer? Look no further than the mirror. You are the creator of sin. Why? Because you are doing what you are doing based upon what you want. Even if you want to help someone, that is you wanting to help someone. Thus, it is a karma-filled action that sets reaction into motion.

We are each born into a world bound by the sins that our parents, our family, and our ancestors have previously committed. We are each defined by the sins of the choices those around us have made.

No person is whole onto himself or herself. But, the one power we have is to limit the sins we individually create. How do we do that? Cast no judgment. Make no decisions for anyone else. Do nothing that has the potential to affect anyone else. Present no opinion. Leave all to be who they are. Let all people think for themselves. Be silent. Be whole. Consciously melt into the cosmic abyss. For it is only from this space of supreme consciousness that no sin is created.

The quest for art has always been a complicated subject. Though it really should not be. Art is understood to be the creative vision of the artist being actualized and brought to life—mind to reality. Certainly, the art that is created in one era is different from the art that is created in another. But, it is each person who creates art that brings his or her mental vision forward into actuality and this is what moves the understanding of art forward.

The problem, (if you want to use this word), with art is, most art is simply mimicking what has happened before. Most people, who live in a specific period of time, simply like a specific type of art that they see and then the few who actually choose to embrace art as a lifestyle set about to recreate that art.

One could question, is this art at all, or is it simply imitation? In the mind of the artist who creates the work, they would, of course, deny any factors of reproduction. But, all one has to do is to look to the new work and then look to other artists from that same time period and it is very easy to see that the majority of creative work is simply a reimagination of what someone else had instigated. Few and far between are the people who actually push the boundaries of art forward. And generally, those who do move the understanding of art forward are the people who are most criticized for what they are creating as it is not yet commonly accepted.

More than simply a place where true inspiration is brought into reality, art has given birth to more reasons for criticism than inspiration. It has given a voice to many a critic. Whereas art, in its truest form, should be a motivating factor to inspire other people to create art, instead, all it predominately does is to allow people to have a vehicle for denunciation. But, the thing to keep in mind at this juncture is that if people are speaking badly about the art, whatever that art may be, then in one way that art has served its purpose as it has motivated people to think, embrace their own emotions, and from this, discuss their interpretation of reality. Yes, what they say may be based in judgment, camouflaged misunderstandings, and even a desire to find a place to launch their own undefined psychological ineptitudes but the art did cause them to think and then to speak so on that level of human consciousness it did serve its purpose.

Most people come at any art they encounter from a perspective of what they have already decided. Most people do not possess the mindset to witness any newness as art. They know what they know they know and that is it.

Most people do not try to create art. Most people do not even think about art unless they are forced to encounter art. Most people only find art as a reason to think, *"I like,"* or, *"I don't like."* Thus, this is what has set the artist apart from the average person of society since the human mind moved to a place where the artist was born.

Once an artist has created art, they are often defined by that art. In the mind of many, what they did then was what they are now. ...Though their now may be motivated and stimulated from a very different place of inspiration. For any of us who have walked down the road of art, we quickly understand that as time moves on, we move on, and our art evolves. What we did then is most likely not what we do now but as our art of the past came to be the first to define the way our art was interpreted that becomes the definition of who and what we are, even though years have past and our consciousness and understandings have evolved greatly.

Again, this takes us to one of the complications of art. What an artist created then may not be what they are creating now but how many people have the aptitude to study an entire body of work instead of simply clinging onto that which is the most debated or most in the public eye?

How do you look at art? How do you interpret art? Do you only see art as something that is defined as art? Or, do you understand that there is art everywhere?

Art is one of the greatest factors of human existence. It is what truly defines a culture, a period of time, and a person—as it is the person who witnesses the art and allows it to emotionally move them in one direction or another.

Art is everywhere, if you allow art to be everywhere. It is there to inspire you. It is even there to provide you with a reason to form judgments. But, at its heart, art exists to allow you to move beyond the judging realms of human reality and transcend into a space where you comprehend that personal inspiration is the ultimate defining factor for the evolution of human consciousness.

03/Jul/2018 07:12 AM

If you encounter the world from a mindset of anger all you will encounter is anger.

If you encounter the world from a mindset of forgiveness and love you will encounter forgiveness and love.

Karuna
02/Jul/2018 07:53 AM

Karuna is the Sanskrit word for compassion. One of the primary tenets of Buddhist practice is the understanding that by encountering the world with a mind set towards embracing compassion you spread the sense of help and betterment to all you encounter.

Compassion is one of the highest states of mind. It is also one of the easiest ones to embrace. Yet, so few people ever put compassion into practice.

Compassion is a frame of mind that possess little or no inter-personal or inter-mental stimulation. Yes, you may feel good when you help someone but making yourself feel good is not the motivation for practicing compassions. The practice of compassion is based upon the spreading of a state of internal caring throughout all of humanity.

As compassion is based upon a mental state lacking obvious stimulation, it is one of the primary practices that promotes meditation. The reason for this is that meditation is designed to calm and silence the mind. To achieve this, the less internal mental noise that must be silenced within the practitioner the better. The more one veers away from mental mind junk stimulated by conflictive behavior the easier a state of true meditation is achieved.

As you think about your life, how much compassion do you practice? How much of your time do you spend turning off your desires, your harsh judgments of others, you conflictive behavior, and actually reaching out to make the lives of other people any better?

Many people falsely believe that by doing their job they may be in the process of helping the betterment of others. But, this is rarely the case. The bartender may make people feel a bit better for a moment but what he or she is serving has the potential to inflict a lot of harm. The comedian may make people laugh but at what cost? What words do they choose to active the laughter in people's mind and how does what they say and whom they use as a comedic tool affect the life of the person they are making smile and the person they are discussing. At best, just like the bartender, they are offering up a momentary fix that has the potential to hurt more lives than it helps.

If you hurt one person you are hurting everyone. That is not compassion.

Those are just two examples of the people who may be fooling themselves into believing that their job performs some means of compassionate help. The fact is, most people do not contemplate and put the microscope on what they are doing and how what they are doing is actually affecting themselves, another person, or the greater whole of the world. They simply do and then make excuses for what they have done.

For example, the martial arts were systems of self-defense born in Asia. Buddhism played an essential role in the evolution of virtually all of these systems of self-defense. Yet, when you look at the average martial arts practitioner, do you find the essence of compassion in what they do or do you find a person who is lost in his or her own ego and is very critical of other practitioners based in their misguided definition of self? They are not practicing the essence of Buddhism. They are not embracing compassion. Thus, they are diluting and distorting the true essence of these arts.

The reason compassion is understood to be one of the greatest human goods is that it witnesses the person who embraces compassion turning off themselves and focusing on the betterment of the someone, the everyone else.

The practice of compassion is simple. Who can you help today? How can you help them today? How can you fix any damage you previously created today? How can you remove the you from the equation and put the them into the primary focus.

The people who have lived the best lives are those who have helped others—those who stopped focusing on themselves and what they wanted and turned the focus onto those in need.

Ask yourself what do you need? How much time do you spend thinking about that need and the methods to obtaining that need? Now, ask yourself, what does that other person need? And, how much more essential is it to their survival in comparison to what you need?

There are a lot of people who actually need help other there. Do you care?

There are a lot of people who could really use your help out there? Are you going to embrace compassion, understand their needs, and reach out a hand of help?

Compassion is simply. You just have to care.

Who do you care about and what are you going to do about it?

Compassion never involves conflict. Compassion is caring, helping, and giving based in the purest sense of these understandings. Can you practice compassion? Can you embrace the highest good?

02/Jul/2018 07:52 AM

Do you ever question your reality?

When You Believe a Lie
30/Jun/2018 07:00 AM

When you hear someone saying something do you ever question who is saying what and why or do you simply believe what you hear? Simply believing what you hear, with no thought, has lead to some of the biggest disasters that this world has witnessed.

Do people lie intentionally? Yes. Do people lie unintentionally? Yes. In either case, what they are saying is not based in the truth and from this a falsehood is spread outwards from one person to the next and onto the next.

People tell lies for all kinds of reasons. Everybody has a reason for saying what he or she is saying. Some people believe they know the facts. Some people want to make their facts, (the facts that only exist in their own mind), a reality. Some people want to cast a judgment and either rise up or diminish another person and to do this they choose words that others listen to and believe.

Why do people lie? There are many reasons for this. Some people are simply pathological liars. They either want to be liked, are liked and want to remained liked, or want to control the thought patterns of other people so they say words that will guide people in this direction.

Some people find an empowerment in altering the facts to suit their own needs. They embrace the sense that people are turning to them for guidance and they find that by created a world dominated by what they think, be it factual or false, they are able to control the thought patterns of other people.

Some people are simply ashamed of what they have lived, what they have done, and from this they are instinctively guided to telling lies. They want to hide the truth.

The people who speak the loudest are generally the liars. The people who talk the most are generally the lairs. The people, who talk about other people, but rarely about themselves, are generally the lairs. The people who boast are generally the lairs. The people who tell people what they think are generally the liars.

Have you ever had someone tell a lie about you? Have you ever had someone alter the facts of reality so it affected your life advancement? What happened to you because of their telling a lie? What happened to them because of their telling a lie?

Have you ever told a lie about someone? Have you ever altered the facts about the truth of a situation in order to affect the life advancement of someone else? If you have you understand the motivation for concocting a lie. What did that concoction result in? Did you gain what you wanted? If you did, what was the price to the life of the other people? What was the price to your life evolution? And, do you care?

Telling the truth is a conscious choice. Telling the truth is not always pretty. Telling the truth may help everyone. Telling the truth may help someone else while it hurts you. But, if you do not tell the truth then the all of your everything is only based in a lie. If your life is based in a lie, you can never be whole. You can never not worry that someone will find out the truth. If you live in this space—if you have to argue to make others believe your truth then you hold no truth.

Question who is saying what and why. Know the truth.

I Forgot To Take My Painting To the Art Show
26/Jun/2018 04:05 PM

A month or so ago this art gallery contacted me and asked me to bring in a few of my Buddha Paintings for an art show they were going to have. Initially I told them I'd think about it. But, they insisted. So, I told them I would bring them one.

Now, to explain my trepidation… Way back in the way back when, I had a person who represented my art. The first thing you realize when you start selling art in art galleries is that the gallery and, *"Your person,"* get like ninety percent of the money. You get very little. Now… Some people don't care. They want their art out there and to them the fame is enough. But, for any of us (like me) who enjoying going to thrift stores and flea markets, you quickly come to realize how much of the art, true artists create, ends up in the donation pile. Finally, at one point, I just said forget it. Sure, I still love to paint and create art but I gave up trying to be a famous artist long ago.

Every now and then, however, like in this situation, I get asked…

Okay, they asked me to bring them the painting on this specific day so that they would have the time to arrange the paintings, of the various artists, in the gallery in lieu of their show. Dumb shit me, I forgot. I had the painting picked out. It was sitting on top of a cabinet. But, life, time, things to do, and the general chaos of life got in the way. I forgot. I did not bring them the painting.

Instead of calling me to remind me or anything nice and normal like that, today I get this

123

very rude email telling me what a horrible person I am, how they will never show my art, and how I will never make it as an artist. Of course, this made me laugh. Now, some people may be very intimidated, hurt, or insulted by these comments but for me it all goes to show how so many people live in the world of the they are the more than everyone else and they hold the keys to the kingdom. ...A kingdom that some of us just don't care about entering. So, oh well, I guess there went my shot. All because of me forgetting to bring this gallery my painting I will never be living the leisurely high life of making millions of dollars per painting. Damn, what am I going to do now?

The Do That You Do and Who You Do It To
25/Jun/2018 02:35 PM

As we are in the midst of the #metoo and the #blacklivesmatter era, I think it is very interesting to observe how the world, at least here in the West, is attempting to force a change onto society, societal norms, and the way in which people behave towards one another. If you study history, you will easily understand that every now and then there comes to be a forced change onto a society. Though this is not necessarily a bad thing, there are a number of unnecessary casualties that result due to the upheaval.

In the past, I've spoken about how the #metoo movement has allow a certain subgroup of people to cast accusations towards a person and then that person has suffered the consequences— guilty without a trial. And, this is still going on. … It's an easy way to get back at someone you're pissed off at.

In not a dissimilar manner, some people have been called out due to their apparent racism. Most recently, Laura Ingalls Wilder (author of among many other titles, Little House on the Prairie). Her name was recently removed from the award previously given in her honor due to her apparent racism in some of her literature.

I do not support racism in any manner but I do believe that we must keep all things in context. When and where she lived was a very different time in history. What people believed, what people said, and what they practiced was very different from what it is now. Look at some of the works of

Samuel Clemens AKA Mark Twain; they were blatantly racist. That's not good. But, that was the mindset of then, not now. I believe you can truly learn a lot about history if you read the literature from any given period of time because it allows you to view how people actually thought.

As I've spoken about many times in the past, where and how I grew up I experienced a lot of reverse racism. I mean, let's get the facts straight. My ancestors had nothing to do with American slavery. My family was still in Scotland throughout that time in history. Yet, me being white, I was often blamed for a lot of the going-ons of that era. But, none of that was anywhere near my fault. Not to mention that I was just a kid. Yet, I was blamed. I was blamed because of the color of my skin. Isn't that racism?

It was like when over the weekend the African-American congresswoman when on her screaming rant telling her constituents to harass any member of the Trump administration they may encounter all based upon the fact that a restaurant would not serve the Press Secretary. But, even if you don't agree with someone or what they stand for that attitude is just wrong. First of all, there is enough craziness and badness in the world. No one should motivate people to take negative actions and/or think negative thoughts. How is what she was suggesting any different from the harassment the African-Americans encountered during the Jim Crow era? All of that kind of stuff is just not right and people should immediately be told to, *"Stop it,"* when they speak in that manner. Where are the people chastising that congresswoman for her hate speak?

To take this subject a bit farther, in this era of casting blame and calling out people for saying and doing the wrong thing, equaling the redefining of cultural norms, it has really surprised me that this new culture has not taken hold on the internet in a more positive fashion. I mean, the internet still seems to be all about judgment and negativity and no one is ever held to task for their bad behavior. Where is the cultural upheaval? Where is the forced changed? Why aren't the people being called out for saying bad things or spreading false propaganda?

I believe that any of us who have been on the dark side of an attack can relate to the fact that some people base their judgments on nothing more than their own personal determinations with little need for actually researching the facts in any true and definitive manner. Even when you explain to some of these people that they are wrong about what they are saying, do they listen? Generally not. Do they say they are sorry and correct their factual inaccuracies? Almost never. And, here lies the problem with all of this redefinition of culture. It is highly based on one person saying one thing and other people not possessing the mental fortitude to find out the facts for themselves and then correct the person who originally spoke what they spoke, saying what they said. Moreover, some people find fame and, thus, a personal sense of self-reward by saying things about other people—particularly if they are inflammatory. I won't go into all of the psychological reasons for this as I am sure I have discussed them in the past. But, people don't care

127

who they hurt because they do not receive any consequences. When they want to hurt someone, they want to hurt someone. And, no matter what their motivation is, hurting that person gives them a sense of empowerment. Maybe it even gives them some money. But, if what they are saying is negative, if what they are saying is untrue, if what they are saying is hurting someone's life, how is that any different from the men who accost women in an inappropriate manner? How is that any different from the damage down by racist behavior? It is the same!

Did all the people who gave me shit back in the day—a white kid in the hood, ever care about the hurt they inflicted on my life. Probably not. Why? Because they were not taken to task. They were not called-out on it. They suffered no consequences. In fact, among their friends, they were cheered. And, this goes to the sourcepoint of all of this bad behavior. People need to be called-out if they are saying or doing something negative or wrong. No matter what their position, no matter what their motivation, they need to be told to stop. But, so many of them who are not bothering women or being racist are simply allowed to spew negativity, particularly on the internet, and never pay a price for the damage that they have unleashed. Is that right? Is that how life should be lived? I think we can all agree the answer to that is, no.

If you are going to take part and try to make the world a better place; first of all, you need to start with yourself—turn off the hatred, turn off the negativity, turn off the judgment, and turn off the misconstrued understanding that you feel you have the right to judge or damage the life of anyone. Next, find out the facts for yourself. Never simply believe something because someone else is saying it. Finally, whenever you see negative words being spoken or negative deeds being done, be strong enough to tell the people who are doing it to stop hurting anyone/everyone. The minute you encounter it, tell them to stop. For all damage to a person's life, no matter how large or how small, begins with one person saying or doing one thing. They need to be told to stop it. If you can't follow these simply understandings don't believe or claim you are helping with the betterment of anything.

What are you doing? Are you a part of the change for betterment? Or, are you simply unleashing your misdirected anger instead of coming to terms with your own inner-meaning?

25/Jun/2018 09:20 AM

The people who don't care will never care.

The people who care will always care.

Who do you want to be and who do you want to be aligned with?

25/Jun/2018 08:50 AM

Do you ever look back to something negative your said or something bad you did to a person one year ago, five years ago, or ten years ago?

What impact did it have on the life of that person?

What impact did it have on your life and your ongoing evolution?

Did it make their life, your life, or the life of anyone else any better?

If you do not think about these actions, if you do not care about these actions, if your do not chart your life actions and their repercussions, you can never understand the evolution of your life and why you encounter the things that you do.

Take a Moment to Appreciate
25/Jun/2018 07:25 AM

Wherever you find yourself in your life right now take a moment to appreciate. Right here, right now, stop and embrace your blessings—feel the perfection.

Maybe you are warm when it is cool outside. Maybe you are cool when it is hot outside. Maybe you have a roof over your head, food in your stomach, and maybe even someone who loves you. For all of these things take a moment and be happy for what you have.

Maybe your boyfriend just broke up with you, maybe you are unhappy with your job, maybe you need a fix, but for this moment, step away from the pain and angst, and stop. Embrace the aliveness you possess right now. Understand the perfection of this moment that you have the ability to feel. For without life you would have nothing.

Everybody has a reason to think about something else. Pretty much everybody wants something else. All that being understood, right now you have something good, you are something real; stop and feel it and appreciate it.

Many people never take the time to appreciate what they have. Do you?

Try it. Take this moment and simply focus on and be happy for the things that you love in your life and the things and the people who take care of you. Feel the something good of this moment.

The great thing about making this a practice that you do everyday is that it spreads out from the moment you think about it further onto your life.

The more you appreciate the more things that you can appreciate come into your life.

Think good thoughts, stop the negativity, and everything becomes better. Be appreciative.

The Thing That You Don't Do
But You Should Do
24/Jun/2018 08:34 AM

Have you ever had the experience of expecting somebody to do something for you but they did not? Maybe it was wishing you a, *"Happy birthday,"* maybe it was inviting you to their wedding, maybe it was inviting your over to watch the game, maybe it was just checking in to say, *"Hi."* You expected it. All logic pointed to them doing it. But, they did not. Now what?

Life is an interesting process of self-motivated ideas tempered by the need to act appropriately to those you are close to and/or know. This life-practice spreads out from that point to behaving in a kind manner to those on the peripheries your existences and onto those you do not even know but encounter as you pass through your life. The main point to keep in mind, while navigating all of this, is that people have feelings and as they have feeling they are affected by the way in which you behave towards them. Thus, if you do not reach out that hand of acknowledgement, relationships may become damaged and feelings may become hurt. What does this equal in the long term? That depends on each individual and their understanding of relationships. But, the one thing that is for sure, feelings may be hurt. And, as feelings make up much of our existence, relationships may be affirmed or destroyed.

How do you behave towards people? Do you take other people into consideration as you pass through life? Do you take their feelings into consideration? Do you continually extend that hand of friendship? Do you think about them or do you only think about yourself?

As we each are unique individuals with our own mind, our own personality, and our own set of life-understandings, we are defined by those elements. This being said, that does not mean that we each are not able to expand our realms of interpersonal understanding and decide to think about the other person as well as ourselves.

In life, many people project their own sense of life-understanding onto other people. Meaning, they make decisions for that person. They assume what they think they feel and what they think they want. But, by doing this, all they have accomplished is to put their own definition onto that person. They have not truly considered their feelings. They have not questioned their feelings on a subject. They have not allowed them to choose to be who they are. They have not allowed them to make a personal choice to do or not do any specific event. Thus, they have made up their mind for them. From this, much of the problems of the world's interpersonal relationships are given birth to.

So, think about it, do you think about other people? Do you remove your own projected definitions that you have constructed about them? Do you allow them to be who they are? And, in doing so, do you reach out to them the way family, friends, and caring individuals actually do? Or, do you just decide for them? Leaving them and you with what? Mostly, what is left is hurt feelings and the question of why do people not care when they really should to care.

Process Verses Experience
22/Jun/2018 07:38 AM

The spiritual path is about process—knowing why you do what you do and doing it very consciously. Life is about experience. The problem with experience is, however, that it is experimental —you are doing things simply to do it, simply because you feel like doing it but from this is born an entire life landscape of emotions, desires, unfulfilled desires, repercussions, and karma.

Why do you do what you do? Do you know why you do what you? Do you care about why you do what you do? Do you think about what you do before you do it? Or, do you simply do? If you live your life based upon the philosophy of the ladder then you enact all kinds of waves actions for what you are doing is affecting not only your own life in an undefined manner but also the lives of all people who encounter your actions.

The difference between the person who truly walks the spiritual path and the person who does not is the fact of caring. The person on the spiritual path cares and from this caring they evaluate their actions before they are taken; they contemplate how their actions will affect other people. If they find them to be detrimental to any person they choose not to do them. Thus, not only does their life remain in a more refined state but they do not damage or hinder the life of any other person who may be impacted by what they do.

Think about how your life has been affected by the unconscious actions of others. Think about how your life has been affected by the conscious actions of others. The one common factor is that your life was affected by what someone else did. You did not do it, yet your were affected because another person's actions encompassed you and your life. Thus, memory, focused emotions (good or bad), and/or counteractions were set into motion. The cycle of actions and reactions become never ending.

A good life is defined by focused positive actions. The only way you can live a life defined by focused positive actions is to consciously evaluate what you are about to do and why you are about to do. You need to understand your why and know the reason for your why. If you want your life to be better—if you want other people's lives to be better, if you want the world to be better then you need to think about other people first, how other people will be affected by your actions and consciously choose to only do good things that helps but never hurts.

Actions in the Echo Chamber
20/Jun/2018 08:08 AM

In this life, all actions have a reaction. Everything you do equals something else. As much as people want to hide from this fact and pretend that it is not the truth, a person's actions always catch up to them.

The reason I speak about this subject so frequently is that I am very commonly questioned by people who are dissatisfied with their life or frustrated by the fact that they have not achieved what they hoped to achieve in life. They want to know why they are stuck where they are stuck in their life. First of all, as I always say, if you have no desires then all of your desires are fulfilled. You are free. But, few people are able to let go of what they want out of life. From this, one must further investigate why they find themselves where they find themselves in life and why something is lacking.

Many people believe that they can hide from the actions they have unleashed if no one sees them perform those actions. But, think about the world today. People live on the internet. But, all actions performed on the internet are being followed by the abstract mind of Big Data. Moreover, for those with the skillset, they can easily tack down who has done what. They simply need to be given the motivation to do so.

There are cameras everywhere. Security cameras are recording everything/all the time. Most of us have security cameras in our homes watching over all those who encroach on our living space. In

139

times gone past, people could do things to where a person lived and get away with it. No longer. People are seen. Their faces are recorded and kept in the cloud for eternity. All that is needed is a reason to expose who they are.

Pretty much everybody has a cellphone. Think about all of the crazy things that are broadcast on the news by people who recorded the bad actions unleashed by somebody who thought what they were doing was unseen.

The fact being the fact, you can no longer do and not be known for your doing. But, that should not be your motivation, guiding you towards doing what you do. Your motivation should be that you are consciously doing good things and never knowingly doing bad things.

Think about it… When somebody has done something nice for you, how did that make you feel? Good, I would imagine. From that nice action, you were probably motivated to do nice things and perhaps be kind to and help other people.

Now, think about when someone has done something bad to you. How did that make you feel? Very negative, I would suppose. How long did you feel negative about that action and that person? Probably for as long as that action affected you. Thus, that action reverberated for an untold period of time in your life. And, throughout that time, it was causing reactive actions to occur to the person who originally instigated it.

As it is commonly understood, all negative deeds a person performs are based upon unrequited anger. If a person is mad at themselves… If a person is mad at the world… If a person is unfulfilled or unhappy… They expound misdirected anger. Instead of getting in touch with themselves and understanding why they are feeling the way they are feeling, they unleash this anger and dissatisfaction onto others. And, here is where the entire sourcepoint for the fall of humanity is given birth to. One person doing one thing.

Many people are so misdirected that they do not think and/or care about the affect they are having on another person or this life-space in general by the actions they take. They just act. For some, if they are living a good life and are more or less content with what is going on in their life, they may even feel good about unleashing negative actions directed towards another person or group. But, life is never about only what occurs in a particular moment. Life is about what occurs down the road due to the action(s) you took in that moment way back when. If your actions have hurt someone—if you actions are still hurting someone, what do you think is going to happen to you? Maybe not today but tomorrow?

Life is an echo chamber. Your life reverberates what you say and what you do. What are you doing?

So, whenever anyone asks me questions— questioning where they find themselves in life, I tell them to go back to the beginning, look at what they have done, who it affected, and what echo has it caused to reverberate farther down the line.

You want to find the person at fault for you feeling what you are feeling/for you experiencing what you are experiencing, look no further than yourself. And, when the hammer falls on you a bit father down your lifeline, look back to the day you did what to whom, way back in the way back when.

The Spiritual Essence

How much time to you spend thinking about god? How much time do you spend thinking about how you can make yourself a more spiritually refined person in order to serve god better? How much time do you spend meditating in order to more consciously join yourself with the interworking's of the cosmic sphere and come to understand and serve the universe in a more productive manner? How much time do you spend putting your own thoughts and desires aside so that you can actually help other people? If you are like most people, you spend virtually no time doing any of this. It is for this reason that those who choose to walk the spiritual path are not only few and far between but are both revered and condemned for their predilection.

What do you want for your life? What are you willing to do to get what you want for your life? How much of what you want for your life is only about you and how much of what you want for your life involves you walking the path towards selfless service and god consciousness?

As most people never think about focusing their life upon understand the god concept. As most people spend virtually no time at all thinking about anything but achieving their personal desires. Few ever question why there is an essential emptiness in their being—that they are always wanting but never feeling truly whole and fulfilled.

It is easy to want what you want. Everybody does that. But, by the very definition of wanting

143

there is developed the addiction of wanting more. The wanter never truly has.

It is easy to think what you think. Everybody does that. But, by thinking without first refining your consciousness, your thoughts are only based upon your perceived projection of reality. They are simply based upon what you personally like and what your personally don't like. The problem with thinking in this manner, though pretty much everybody does it, is that all you are doing is adding conflict to not only your own mind, because everything out there is not going to be the way you want it to be, but you will also be adding conflict to the greater all as some people will agree with you while others will not. From this, all that is born is ongoing personal and external disagreements that do nothing for the greater landscape of life but create struggles, leading to skirmishes, leading to war.

Without interpersonal self-awareness based upon the understanding that personal desire will never be truly fulfilled and personal opinions and judgments are nothing more than just that, a person's life is defined by nothing more than lacking what they truly want and seeking fleeting empowerment to get that something that they will never truly have. From this, a life of dissatisfaction and destruction is given birth to.

Few people choose to walk the spiritual path and embrace their own spiritual essence. Most who do walk the spiritual path are drawn to it by some unexplainable something that emanates from within themselves. A few intellectually understand why spirituality is better than mindless materialism and force themselves to redefine their life. But, if one does not understand the benefits of embracing the greater concept of this universe and helping others before they help themselves then all one does is walk a life path defined by selfishness.

Life is defined by the realities of life. We all need a place to live, we all need food to eat and water to drink. But, how we get those reality-based necessities and what we think about and how we behaving while meeting those life-essential needs defines who we are, what we are giving back to the greater whole of this world and the universe, and whether or not we are walking on the spiritual path.

You can dismiss spiritually as most people do. But, you cannot deny that the spiritual person provides more to this ever-evolving life space then the person who only thinks about themselves. Moreover, the person walking the spiritual path does so while existing with a purer, more conscious set of life standards, while embracing a state of inner calm than does the average person who only thinks about themselves.

So, who do you want to be? What legacy do you want to create? How do you want to feel as you pass through your life? This is your life. That question can only be answered by you. Do you want to embrace your spiritual essence?

The Remembering Mind

Most of your life is based upon what you remember. In fact, even as you read this essay, most of your deliberation of what you have read is based in the past tense. You read it but what you read is being translated by your mind into a way you can understand and/or agree or disagree with it. Your reading is in the now but that now passes so quickly it is not until it has been read that you have the chance to understand it. Thus, all understanding is based in the cognitive process of remembering.

We each live what we live in the moment to the best degree that we can. But, it is the memories we hold that come to define our life understanding, our overall life experience, and, thus, how we behave. We are entirely defined by our memories.

For each of, we hold some memories dear to our heart. When we think about those memories they make us happy. Each of us also holds memories that cause us pain when they are remembered. Hopefully, those memories are fewer then the ones that make us smile but virtually all of our memories are given to us by someone else. Someone else chose to do something that either made us happy or made us angry or sad.

Some memories are completely blocked from our mind. For those of us who have experienced trauma, we understand that we are told that we lived through something but we have no actual memory of it. This action has been documented as the way the mind blocks out intense physically or emotionally painful experiences. In

146

recent years there have been studies done in order to develop techniques and medications to help people block out or at least substantially diminish traumatic memories from their mind. At some point, these methods will most likely come to be fully functional and, from this, some people may be able to find relief from hurtful memories that haunt them. These developing methods can and will never actually remove the fact of the experience, however, but as they will not be remembered the question then can arise, if the person does not remember the experience, did that experience actually happen?

Good or bad, all shared memories are brought about by the interaction of one or more people. The majority of people do not think about this however. They simply live their life, doing what they want to do. They simply act. If their doing makes someone happy, they too may be happy. If their doing makes someone sad, do they care? Some do. But, many do not. In fact, there is a certain subset of people who set out to hurt other people and once they do that they take pride in their actions; telling others about said actions. Is this right? For most of us, the answer to that question would be, *"No."* But, does this change the behavior of these people? Absolutely not. As long as a person is embolden in their actions and receiving no negative response to their actions, they do those actions and, in fact, may take pride in them once they are cast to memory.

For each of us, memory is the defining factor of our life. As we each think all day, everyday, our memories make up a good percentage of our thought process. Due to the interactive

147

action(s) of others, some possess a lot of positive memories while other are forced to be defined by negative memories brought about by the actions of someone else.

In life, we each experience and interpret situations in our own unique way. The actions that may cause one person to emerge with a positive memory will cause another person to remember it from a very negative perspective. This too is one of the defining factors of life.

At the root of all memories is what we have personally chosen to do, delineated by what we were capable of doing and allowed to do, as we interacted with others during the timespan of living our life. As we are each responsible for the memories of other people, we should each enter into all life interactions in the most conscious and caring manner possible. For, what we do, creates the memories that others will hold. If we hurt someone/anyone that memory will be the definition of our life in the mind of that person forever. Is that how you want to be remembered?

Live consciously. Always take the other person into consideration. Only do good things that will create good memories in the mind of other people. For how we are remembered is the only true definition of our life.

*   *   *

17/Jun/2018 01:34 PM

The measure of your honor and your integrity is defined by the way you behave when there is no one there to observe you.

17/Jun/2018 08:50 AM

As long as you blame someone else for doing what you do you will never understand the essence of life.

*   *   *

17/Jun/2018 08:24 AM

If you don't understand that your actions of hurting someone or something, for any reason, are sinful, then you are the ultimate sinner.

*   *   *

17/Jun/2018 08:24 AM

Stop making excuses for doing what you do.

You did it, you are responsible.

*   *   *

17/Jun/2018 08:24 AM

You can never be forgiven for your sins until you have rectified your sins.

153

Religious Spirit Religious Form
17/Jun/2018 08:15 AM

Many people, most of the world in fact, define themselves by what religion they follow. *"I am a Christian." "I am a Jew." "I am a Hindu." I am Buddhist." "I follow Islam,"* and so on. They are a believer.

In each religion there is a prescribed set of practices—a group of techniques that each follower is expected to practice. As we all understand, most people may follow a certain percentage of those practices but most fall far short from performing them in the manner in which they were designed. At best, most people add their own set of definitions to these practices so that they can do what they want and get away with their own inadequacies.

As a believer, most people fall into a pattern of belief, defined by what they were indoctrinated into as a child. They did not so much choose their religion; their religion chose them by what culture they were born into. Some people, however, move away from their original religious indoctrination and transition forward onto believing something else. Though the focus of their belief may have changed, their life is still defined by what they believe. They are still a believer.

No matter what religion a person follows, as a believer, they are defined by their beliefs. What they believe defines who they are and what they do.

As most people redefine their own personal understanding of the fundamental practices of their religion, they adapt them to crate an excuse for their shortcomings. How many people do you know, who actually claim a religion, and define themselves as being a part of that religion, do not sway from the true teachings of that religion in how they behave towards other people and life on the grad scale?

Within virtually all formalized religions is taught the higher truth of living a life defined by a positive interaction with people, life, and the environment by not stealing, not hurting, not killing, and doing good things to help the greater all as opposed to simply encountering life in a selfish and unthinking manner.

Do you consider yourself a religious person? Do you claim a particular religion as you own? If you do, how much of what you do, what you say, and how you treat other people and other living creatures is defined by what is truly taught in your religion?

As the modern era came upon us, many people rebuked their religion and claimed to be a non-believer. By claiming this, they attempted to free themselves from the dogma and the demands of their religion. But, did they truly become a non-believer? If you know one of these people, if you watch them through their life and as they approached the end of their life, you will see that though they claimed the mantel of non-belief when they needed something that was not being provided to them within the realms of the material world they quickly refocused their mind into the state of a believer. Thus, from this example alone, we can quickly understand that there are virtually no true non-believers. Everybody believes in something. Some just attempt to claim the opposite.

With this as an understanding, this means that we all are a person of religion. We all are believes. As we all are believes, this belief should dominate what we do and how we do it. Thus, we should all stop making excuses to ourselves and to the world on the whole about the things we say, the things we do to other people, and to the world as a whole.

As you are a believer. Believe what your teachings teach. Stop making excuses. Stop hurting people. Stop hurting other living creatures. Stop hurting the world.

17/Jun/2018 08:04 AM

Stop passing the blame for what you do.

Whatever you do, for whatever reason you do it, you are responsible.

17/Jun/2018 07:09 AM

How often do you listen to what the birds have to say?

17/Jun/2018 07:07 AM

When you've done something wrong and you refuse to admit that you've done something wrong does that mean that you did nothing wrong or simply that you refuse to admit that you did something wrong?

The Combative Mind

Why is it that some people encounter all life interactions as an attack, for which they counter attack? Do you?

Have you ever observed this process? Someone will say something and some other person will pounce. They will attack the words, the person, the person's character, the person's life and/or lifestyle. Maybe they personally know the person, maybe they have never met the person, but from what one person says another person attacks.

Maybe this person is not even speaking anything negative or argumentative. Maybe they are simply saying something that they see to be positive. Maybe they are simply revealing a portion of their life that brings them joy, yet someone else; someone out there finds that action to be a causation factor to attack.

Have you ever attacked in this manner? Have you ever been attacked in this manner?

There are certain groups of people where this mindset is widespread. Certainly in sports, the martial arts, (as I have detailed extensively), onto politics, and even religion. Why is so prominent in these groups? Because within these groups people base their substance upon belief. But, as I have long stated, belief does not make something universally true, it just makes it a belief. But, belief fuels conflict.

More than being solely defined by a group, this mindset is personally activated within the mind of an individual. Some people simply want to attack. They especially want to attack when they can do so from afar. For then, no physical conflict is eminent. But, this is not always the case. At the root of this enacted, unnecessary conflict is the mind of an individual calling out, *"I know more than you. I am more than you."* But, are they?

For those of us who choose to live in a space of peace, we clearly understand that people who involve themselves in the mindset of attack are instigating it from a position of personally developed self-worth and/or personal insecurity and inadequacy. For a person who is full and aware and true to their own mind does not need to project their beliefs onto anyone else. They know what they believe they know and knowing that they know is enough for them.

Most of us do not want to fight. Most of us do not want conflict brought into our life. We separate ourselves from those people who embrace this mindset. Unfortunately, those who embrace the mind of conflict are all around us and, sometimes, these people try to drag us into their warzone. Then, there's not a whole lot we can do about it except do our best to ignore them.

But, think about life... When are you the happiest? Are you the most content when you are doing happy things that makes you and the people around you feel good? Or, are you invigorated by conflict? If your mind takes you to embracing the ladder, all I can say is, you should really keep that stuff to yourself for it only hurts the overall niceness of the world. And, nice is always better than not nice.

Peace is a great space to exist within. Conflict is based upon unresolved interpersonal anger. Who do you want to be? Happy or angry?

If you choose to, you can get you mind right if you are angry and are one of those people who invokes conflict. You just have to work on it. Why don't you try? The next time you see or hear something where you would normally pounce. Stop yourself. Turn your internal judgment and anger into understanding—understanding that we all are who we are. And, if you don't like what a particular person is saying—if don't like what who and what they are claiming, be more than the lower self you used to embrace and step away and do something that makes you and everybody else happy.

Do not create conflict. Do not embrace the conflict instigated by others. Choose peace. Then, everything becomes better.

Bạn có thể lắng nghe cái mà người khác đã nói về Niết Bàn.

Bạn có thể tôn thờ họ là những người hiểu biết vĩ đại.

Nhưng, nếu bạn chỉ hành động như thế mà thôi, bạn chưa bước vào con đường đưa tới Giác Ngộ Bản Thân, bạn chỉ bước trên con đường của một kẻ sùng đạo.

Sự giác ngộ chỉ tới khi bạn ngưng đóng vai làm một đệ tử và khởi sự làm một người tự giác cho chính bản thân mình.

Vietnamese translation of a passage from the Vietnam edition of Nirvana in a Nutshell.

163

Do You Have the Right to Have an Opinion?
13/Jun/2018 08:59 AM

If you ask the average person in the Free World is they have the right to have an opinion, their answer is obviously going to be, *"Yes."* They have the right to think what they want, feel what they want, and tell everyone else about the way they think and feel. The problem with this whole scenario is, however, that most people never ask themselves the question, *"Why do I feel the way I feel and how is what I feel going to affect someone else when I express my opinion to other people about that feeling?"*

In many ways, opinions are used as a weapon. They are used as a tool to hurt a person or perhaps a business that a specific individual does not like. Yes, opinions also can help a person or a business, but it seems that it is always the most self-motivated and mis-directed individuals that speak the loudest when they express the way they feel.

Think about some of the opinions you currently hold. Think about your opinion about a person you know, a band you listen to, a sports team you watch, a business you go, or a whatever... Do you ever truly question why do you feel the way you feel about that certain something? Sure, you may like a person or you may hate a person, you may like the music a band plays or you may hate the music a band plays, you may like a business or you may be mad at them because they did not treat you the way you wanted to be treated, but beyond all that, what is the deeper motivation that caused you to arrive at your opinion based conclusion in the first place? What caused you to initially interact with that entity? And, why do you want to express your opinion about that person or thing in the first place? …Those are important points; take a moment to think about them.

Sure, there is a lot of karma associated with possessing an opinion. I don't want to get all abstract and philosophical here but think about it, when you express your opinion about someone or something to someone else; you are guiding that person in their thinking. From that very example alone you must understand that what you say has consequences as you are affecting the way other people will view that person or thing. Thus, you are setting your karma into motion.

Most people don't think about this. They don't care. They just want to think what they think and say what they want to say. The person or the business they are talking about is not them, so they do not truly care what affect they are having on them. But, what this really tells us is that the person who expresses opinions, especially those who do so in a meaningless or hurtful fashion, does not possess the ability to take the other person into consideration. They do not consciously comprehend that they too are a person and they too have feelings, and, that any business, team, or band, they speak about is made of people who have feelings. They do not care that by expressing an opinion they are affecting the life of that person or persons.

Again, opinions are often used as a weapon. Thus, many of the people who express them want to hurt a person or persons. But, this takes us back to the entire motivation for using opinions as a life tool in the first place. If you do not do it consciously, if you have not truly analyzed why you have your opinion about that person or that thing in the first place, then you are simply living a life defined by generating karma that will come back at you as you are not aware enough to realize that your words are a weapon.

Understand yourself. Know why you hold the opinions that you do. Contemplate how your opinions will affect someone else. Choose to understand that simply because you feel something that does not make what you feel a universal truth.

Every word you speak evokes repercussions. Think before you speak.

12/Jun/2018 09:23 AM

Sometimes you create interesting variables in your life.

Sometimes you are handed interesting variables in your life.

The only problem with possessing interesting variables is then you have to make a choice.

A choice is what sets the rest of your life into motion.

What choice will you make?

The Good That You Do
12/Jun/2018 07:30 AM

What are you planning to do good for someone today? If you are like most people, you woke up thinking about your job, your relationship, your friends, your upcoming vacation, checking your email, or looking at kitten videos on Instagram. You thought about all kinds of things but you did not think about what could you do good for someone else.

When most people wake up in the morning, whatever thought that was prominent in their mind when they went to sleep is what first comes to mind. If you were angry, unhappy, sad, or heartbroken, that is the first thought you encounter. If you were happy, joyous, or in love that is the first thought that comes to mind. But, most of life isn't like that. Most of life is defined by the commonality of the everyday. This is a good thing because negative emotions lead to negative actions, just as positive emotions lead to positive actions. But, actions always lead to the something else, particularly when they are based upon intense emotions.

Going to sleep is a time of release. If there are no impactful emotions in your mind before sleep, you commonly wake up to a mind free, rested, and able to encounter new and insightful thinking. Yes, that is where habits takes over, like: thinking about your job, your relationship, your friends, your upcoming vacation, checking your email, or looking at kitten videos on Instagram. But, it is also a time when new thought patterns and new

168

ideas are given birth to. It is a time to try something new.

Let's get to the ideology of doing something good... Again, when you woke up this morning what were you planning to do good for someone today? Now that you are awake and consciously thinking, what are you planning to do good for someone today? If you do not have that plan in mind, you should start rethinking your life and your life patterns because, think about it, doesn't doing something good make you feel good—doesn't doing something good for someone else also make them feel good. Thus, doing something good is the perfect equation.

Due to the definitions of life, many people find themselves angry with someone. Maybe it is their boss, a lover who jilted them, someone who cheated them, on down to something ridiculous like an actor, a musician, or someone on a sports team that they don't like. People want to fill their mind with emotion. They do this because they do not have anything better to think about. But, what does any of that emotion equal? What does saying or doing something negative, based upon that emotion, equal? Nothing good, that's for sure. To act on those emotions only enhances, focuses, and spreads those emotions which never ends in anything good.

Here's what I suggest, if you find yourself unhappy with or angry at someone, do something good for them, say something nice about them. Make their life a little bit better. I am sure if you do this you will immediately see the power of doing something good and then you can start to understand how the doing of something good

169

always makes the anything and the everything just a little bit better.

So, who are you planning to do something good for today?

*   *   *

11/Jun/2018 09:40 AM

Most people don't tell the truth.

Zen Filmmaking:
Beyond The Roller Blade Seven
09/Jun/2018 09:47 AM

As I frequently discuss, hardly a week goes by that someone does not contact me about *The Roller Blade Seven* and wants to discuss some aspect of that Zen Film. Which is great! That's fine! I get it... It's a bizarre film. And, that is exactly what we had in mind when we created it. Though, in all honesty, that was never the vision I had for my film career when I first entered the industry. But, I've said all this before...

The thing about *Roller Blade Seven* and all the turmoil that surrounded its creation is, so many people see that film and believe that is where *Zen Filmmaking* ended. They think that somehow RB7 is the end-all culmination of *Zen Filmmaking*. It is not. In fact, due to all of the craziness during the Production, the Post Production, and the initial Distribution of RB7, one can conclude that RB7 is anything but true *Zen Filmmaking*. Yes, it is crazy. Yes, it is weird. Yes, we had a lot of fun making it. Yes, it has etched a place for itself in Cult Film History but did *Zen Filmmaking* begin and end with that film? No.

As each production possesses its own set of criteria and definitions, RB7 had its own, as well. And, that is what defines that film. But again, was what took place and what was presented on the screen in that film the end-all of *Zen Filmmaking?* No, not at all. That film just was what that film was. Nothing more, nothing less.

As I always tell everybody, *Zen Filmmaking* is never about the story. …The stories have all been told… *Zen Filmmaking* is about a visual cinematic experience. It is about invoking emotions and thoughts in the mind of the viewer. As each person brings their own set of standards and ideologies to every/any film that they watch, anyone who ever sees a Zen Film will come away with something different. …As they should…

FYI: I haven't made a narrative-driven Zen Film since 2009 so what most people who discuss *Zen Filmmaking* are talking about is actually ancient history.

The fact is, *Zen Filmmaking* is more about philosophy that about actual cinema. And, this is where so many critics and movie watchers get it wrong. It is about embracing a philosophic vision on the screen. As such, even if you project one never-ending single image on the screen, that can be *Zen Filmmaking,* if *Zen Filmmaking* is what you hope to invoke with that single image.

I know there are a couple of film schools that teach courses on *Zen Filmmaking.* Of course, none of them, (at least not yet), have invited me to come and give a seminar or be the actual instructor… But, that's okay. I get it. They want to control the message—even though I am the one invented the message. Yeah sure, I own the Trademark. Yeah sure, I instigated and formalized the understanding. But, like I always say, *"Make it your own…"* You don't have to do what I do to make a Zen Film. You simply have to do what you do.

Zen Filmmaking is about the freedom of naturalness. It is not about following any film formula that I may have used in the past. From this very definition it gives rise to the understanding that there are no definitions. …Not even the definition of no definition. …As isn't that the ultimate understanding of Zen?

So, for all you people out there writing and talking about RB7, remember that was the beginning of *Zen Filmmaking,* it was not the end. It keeps changing. It keeps evolving. So please, don't hold myself, my filmmaking, or other *Zen Filmmakers* locked into that place in time. That was there. That was then. Now, I am here. Where are you?

08/Jun/2018 01:59 PM

As long as what you do doesn't affect me, I don't care what you do. So, why do you care what I am doing?

Seeing What the Camera Sees
But What About When the Camera Doesn't
See It?
08/Jun/2018 07:59 AM

Whenever I teach a class on cinematography or photography I always emphasis the fact that you really must see what the camera sees. You cannot fall prey to the misbelief that the camera is capturing everything in the same manner as you are seeing it or you will most likely end up very disappointed with your captured images. Particularly in the days when cinematography and photography took place on film, you never truly knew what you had until your film was developed. Then, sometimes it was too late. I have told stories about some of the mishaps I have had encountered with some of the films I have worked on in my articles and books on the subject in the past.

Certainly, one of the primary things you must do, whenever you plan to photograph anything, is to know your equipment. You must get out there and shoot things while learning how your camera does what it does and why.

In today's world, so much of the cinematography and photography takes place on your smartphone that many people do not give the craft any thought. They just push a button, capture the image, and that is that. But, even with the ease of this process there are shots that come out, more or less, the way you saw them but there are many that do not.

As most people don't really care about the quality of their cinematography and their photography, their shots don't really matter. But, for those of us who do care, for those of us who actually attempt to create great cinematic and photographic images, we really must take this whole process to heart no matter what level of equipment we are using.

First of all, it is essential to understand, a camera, no matter the price, can and will never capture and image exactly the way your eyes see that image. So, you must understand that fact and then work with that fact. You must come to know your camera and you must come to understand how to make it function as best as possible.

The fact is, in today's photographic climate, you can easily do things with aftereffects, many of which are right on your phone, that would have cost thousands of dollars to achieve just a few years ago. And, that is a good thing. This being said, if you don't capture the image to the best of your ability then altering that image will not create any level of excellence.

To this end, and for any photo or movie you take, pull yourself back from the instantaneousness we have all come to expect in today's digital world and study your camera. Take the time and learn the way it captures images. Learn what in can do and what it can't do. And then, like all of the great cinematographers and photographers work with and work around that fact as best as you can and understand that simply because you are seeing something with your eyes that does not mean that you camera will be able to capture that image in the exact manner as you are seeing it.

See what you see but understand that no one and no thing is going to be able to capture that image exactly the way you are seeing it. Thus, all images are ultimately only seen by you.

07/Jun/2018 04:51 PM

At what point does something stop being hot and start getting cold?

Why Do You Want To Bother People?
07/Jun/2018 10:23 AM

Do you ever sit back and take notice of nature? Do you ever take a moment out of your life and observe your environment? Maybe you see a bird or a squirrel. Do you ever just stop and watch their actions, observer their movement? It's beautiful! When you are doing that, (if you are doing that), do you then think to throw a rock at them simply to mess with their existence? Probably not. They're nature. They're beautiful. So why would you do?

Most people never think to mess with nature. Then why do some people think to mess with other people?

For some reason people want to analyze, criticize, and attack other people. They especially do that when they do not have to bring the attack face-to-face with that other individual. As long as they can do it from a distance, they are safe. Yes, this is the mentality of a coward, but look around the world, this is how most wars are fought. Do the presidents, the dictators, the generals get in the middle of a battle? Nope… They leave that to the foot soldiers to fight the battles they created.

Why do people want to judge other people? Why do people want to criticize other people? Why do people want to attack other people? I will let you answer that question for yourself because I am sure there are any number of valid explanations. But, the fact of the matter is that they do and this is where all the problems of life begin.

180

Think about your life… Have you been analysis, criticized, or attack by someone else? Why did they do it? And, what did it prove? Did it make their life better? Did it make your life better? Or, did it just add to the never-ending chaos and crisis of this world?

People choose to do things because they are allowed to do things. Freedom is great. Freedom of thought is great. Freedom of choice is great. But, what a person chooses to do with that freedom is what sets the stage not only for their life but the life of all those they encounter. If you are a person who throws a rock at a squirrel who is simply living his life and has no way of defending himself as he never saw that rock coming, what does that tell you about who you are, what you are living, and what you are invoking?

Most people are good people. They love nature, they love people, they love life. They attack no one. But, there are those that do. From these people is where all of the damage to the life of other people and to the greater whole of life is given birth to. Yes, most of these people will claim a motivation for throwing that unseen rock. They will blame it on the person they threw that rock at. But, if a person is not psychologically self-aware enough to see that the only reason they are throwing that rock is something emanating from within themselves, then all is lost for they take no responsibility for their actions, simply casting blame to others outside of themselves.

You create the world. You are the one who can look at and love nature or you are the one who can throw the rock and ruin it all.

*   *   *

06/Jun/2018 03:38 PM

It's easy to pretend when nobody knows the truth.

What Else Do You Want?
06/Jun/2018 03:35 PM

It is kind of an interesting situation, I suppose… It is very common that people contact me and ask me for something. The things they ask me for pretty much span the whole gambit of my life but some of the common ones are, "I'm a student and don't have much money can you send me some of your movies or your books?" "I've been an extra in a couple of films and now I want to make my own movie, will you finance it for me?" *"Will you send me a signed photograph?" "I'm an actor, will you put me in one of your films?" "I want to learn how to make a movie, will you hire me and teach me how?" "I want to write a review about one of your movies that I saw on a torrent site on the internet but I don't feel comfortable criticizing you and your film unless I actually own a copy. Will you send me one?" "I've just gotten into VHSs, will you send me some copies of your films on video tape." "I really like your music so I used it to soundtrack my film. Is that okay?"* And, the list goes on…

Now, a lot of people don't even ask, they just take. But, I guess, that is a whole different issue. I mean goddamn, how many of my movies are out there on sites in the dark abyss of cyberspace and people are viewing them for free? Who knows? What I do know is that somebody who had nothing to do with the creation of those films is making money off of them but I am not. …Same with my books and my music. *"Internet piracy is not a victimless crime!"*

183

You know, I get it... Everybody wants everything for free. Some even believe that since they bought a copy of some of my something that they have the right to do whatever they want with it; copyright laws be damned. But, why do you think there are copyright laws in the first place? The answer, to protect the creators.

Everybody has a reason for doing what they are doing. Like I always say, *"Everybody has an excuse."* But, do you ever ask yourself before you ask anybody for anything, *"What can I do for that person?"* Or, do you not even think of and/or about that person? Are you only thinking about what you want? Do you simply want what you want and think that as you want something from them, they must already have the all and the everything that they need?

Life is an interesting process. For some, life is about giving. For others, life is about getting and taking. Who are you? And, what do you try to give anyone?

The Ridiculous Things That People Believe
05/Jun/2018 01:58 PM

As we are now at the fifty-year of point of when Robert F. Kennedy was assassinated, there has been a lot of programming on the radio (and elsewhere) about the man, what he accomplished, and how and when he was as killed; including the various conspiracy theories. I understand that many people, of a certain age, do not even know who he was but I will leave that for you to explore. I will say that the talk of the man has sent me to remembering...

When Bobby Kennedy was assassinated at the Ambassador Hotel in Los Angeles, I lived about two blocks away from that location. When he was killed it was obviously all over the news. The next day at school, we children were talking about it and one of my classmates made the statement that the reason Sirhan Sirhan, (the killer of Bobby Kennedy), was actually arrested was because of the fact that he had two names that were the same. Even as a ten year old, I knew that was a ridiculous statement but many of classmates instantaneously believed him. I think it was right then and right there that I realized you could not believe everything somebody says simply because they say it and they present their false knowledge as a fact.

Think about it... Are you one of the people who believes someone simply because they say something? Or, do you take the time to dig below the surface and find out the truth for yourself?

A lot of people say a lot of things. A lot of people say a lot of things that are untrue.

185

I do not know where my classmate came upon his knowledge. Maybe his parents said it, maybe he heard it from a friend, maybe he just made it up... But, wherever it came from, he spoke it to other people, and other people believed him—believed him even though he was wrong. So, what does that tell you about life—how you live it and who you believe?

Next time you immediately believe somebody simply because they said something, think about this story. Think about what is the source of their knowledge, where and why they came to their conclusions, and then go out and find out the truth for yourself.

Devotion Without Question
05/Jun/2018 08:58 AM

Many people seek something to believe in. As such, they seek someone to believe in. Some find this in the form of interpersonal love: one person to another in one of those forever dreamed about relationships that last forever. Others turn to their desires towards higher ideals; love for a more spiritual something. But, sometimes these two get interchanged and that is where the problems begin.

As most people, from most cultures, are programmed into a mindset that places a high value on religion and, as such, religious teachers, some people are taken in by the words and the deeds of those purported to possess great spiritual knowledge.

In some cases, these are beings that have been dead for centuries. From this, their reputation of spiritual greatness has grown and though no one really knows what they actually said or actually did, their imagined image of perfection has become legendary.

From a psychological perspective, one can debate there are many problems with this process, none-the-less, those religious icons, themselves, can harm no one. It is those who are alive that cause the problems.

As has been so-well documented, a lot of spiritual teachers have claimed to live one lifestyle but have, instead, done just the opposite; especially in terms of their sexuality. Now, if they just called out who and what they were, in this day and age, there would be little problem. They would not be a hypocrite as they were honest about their desires and their lifestyle. Thus, they lived what they preached. But, so few are like that. For some reason, so many of them what to pretend to live a celibate or monogamous life but they fall far from their own projection. Some, when they are caught, ask for forgiveness, others deny; but a lie is a lie is a lie and so what are we left with? A spiritual teacher who lies about who and what they are. Thus, they are not a true spiritual teacher at all? No.

Now, I could speak about all those in the news. But, that is someone else's research and revelations. So, I will talk about what I know and my experiences that pertain to this issue.

My whole life, I have been drawn to eastern spirituality. Thus, when I became a teenager, got a car, and could get out and around, I found my way to Swami Satchidanand's Integral Yoga Institute, where I came to be a very active member and his soundman on the West Coast. For those of you who may not know, in the 1960s, 1970s, and into the 1980s, he was one of those big-players in the Guru Game. He attracted thousands of people to his lectures and he had a large crew of direct disciples. Me, being one of them. All good... He also claimed to be celibate. But, was he?

In the later days of his life, there came to be a lot of accusations about him. But, let's look at the facts. On the West Coast he owned and lived in this beautiful hilltop house in Montecito, California. One of the richest communities in California. I helped to put in the enclosed Jacuzzi into his house. He drove a beautiful 1957 fully restored Cadillac. You know the ones with the big fins. He was a pilot. But, more important and revealing was the fact that a beautiful, very expensively well-dressed, European woman lived with him in his house. Just her and him. His secretary, as she was called. Let's put the numbers to together on that one... What do you think was going on?

For me, I have always been a suspicious person. Due to my life experience(s), I generally don't believe people until they are proven truthful and valid. Did I question his celibacy? Of course, I did. Did it bother me? Not really... That wasn't why I was there. In fact, one of his other disciples, a South Asia man who knew him from India, would tell stories of woman in the guru's presence. Did it bother him? I guess not. Did the other disciples have any questions about the relationship between the secretary and the guru? Nope, they just believed. They believed he was living what he preached. But, blind belief has led to so many problems. But, that's another blog...

...Moreover, I have talked about this issue with Satchidananda in greater length in my books likes, *Zen: Tales for the Journey.* If you're interested...

But, this all goes to what you believe and why you believe it. It goes to what you want out of someone.

Does a person lying make them a liar? Yes, it does. Does lying make a person less of a spiritual being? Absolutely. Should a person lie? Never. Should a spiritual teacher lie? Of course not. For all a lie does is to create a world of liars where everyone who has believed you and believed what you said; you have made become part and parcel to your lie. Thus, they live their life, they believe what they believe, based upon your lie. And, that is just wrong.

The truth be told, of all of the celibate disciple who followed Gurudev, they were all true to their craft. True to the craft until they met someone and left the celibate fold. Me too. But, that's okay. They/me were true to themselves. They took the training seriously. And, they did not lie about anything.

I am certain that most of the people who read this blog have not set their sites on becoming a spiritual teacher. That's good! But, wherever you find yourself in life, you must live in a space of truth. You must not deceive. You must not present the facts in a manner that only makes you look good; for the truth is the truth is the truth. There is no interpretation of it. There is no personalization of it. If you do that, all that makes you is a liar. And, no one likes a liar. For all they ultimately do is mess up the life of everyone they touch. Tell the truth.

We Have To Make Things Right
04/Jun/2018 07:52 AM

In the past year or so there has been so much emphasis placed on outing those men who have done wrong things to woman. Particularly in the film industry, there has been a loud outcry about male dominance and male impropriety but this inappropriate mindset is far reaching and the call for justice has moved onto other areas of life, though far more slowly due to the fact that the people who are speaking in those arenas do not possess so loud a voice. What this tells us it that it is time for a change. It is time to make things right and to stop doing the negative things that have been done in the past. And, this goes for women as well as men.

Of course, there is a downside to all of this. Currently, we have entered into a time where false accusations are rampant but due to the fact that there is so much of the ongoing goings on, there have been more than a few people who have been thrown into the bad action mix that do not belong in that batch. Some accusers have found a means for revenge for being shunned, overlooked, having their emotional advances unrequited, their choices regretted, and/or them just not liking a particular person or not being happy with themselves. So, it is essential to keep in mind that not all of the accused are guilty.

This being said, this entire movement causes us to understand the fact that we all really need to look at who we are, what we do, why we do it, and how what we do affects other people.

191

How much of your time do you spend thinking about how what you do will affect someone else? Ask yourself, do you actually set out to hurt someone, control someone, or hurt or damage his or her existences? Do you care how your actions will affect another person as you pursue your desires? And, do you only care about yourself, how you feel, what you achieve, and everyone else be damned?

What we are currently seeing is an upending to those who have behaved in an uncaring, unthinking, and hurtful manner. Where it will end, only time will tell. But, many of the culprits are being taken to task. And, this is a good thing.

Today, I took a moment and flipped on the TV. There was a scene where a woman was experiencing sexual violence in some bad B-movie on the *El Rey Network*. The first thing I did was to change the channel. But, it did make me think because earlier today I had finally opened the copy of the book I was sent, *The Bad Movie Bible*. Good book! Especially for those of us who have created cinema in that genre or like movies of that type. It is an entertaining reference manual. The author even did a fun review about *The Roller Blade Seven*. I also took note of the review the author wrote about my *Zen Filmmaking* brother, Donald G. Jackson's film, *Hell Comes to Frogtown* where the author references the fact that it was a, *"Sexist movie,"* which it was.

As Don advanced towards his death, he truly embraced his Christianity and he came to truly regret the message he portrayed in some of his films that evoked male dominance and sexual violence, though he always emphasized the fact that it was due to his screenwriter that caused that message to be in the films. Me, I always refused to use any of that kind of storyline in my films. I do not believe that anyone should glorify anything that we all know is wrong and hurts people.

In the case of Don Jackson's films, he created a couple of movies that embellished just that, however. A couple of them are very well liked in the *Cult Film Community.* Don, the filmmaker, came to hate those movies but the audiences still wishes for them to be seen. I tired to follow the wishes of Don and bury those films upon his death but there were so many bootleggers out there trying to release their versions and as I am the sole holder of all Rights, Title, and Interest to those films all I could do to combat someone who had nothing to do with the creation of the films and never even met Donald G. Jackson was to release authorized versions. So, even me, I was sucked into that trap.

Like I questioned of a man who wants to show one of those movies and sell copies of it at a film event he's having, *"Can you really support that style of human behavior? Because I can't."* But, he's going to do what he's going to do because just like most people they do not care how what they do, based upon whatever desire they hold, may hurt someone else, dead or alive, or hurt the overall, greater mindset of the entire world.

…This is the material world and people do what they want to do and they just don't care. They don't care until someone makes them pay for their crimes. And, that is exactly what should happen. You should not hurt people, force people to do

193

things they don't want to do, and not care about the hurt you've inflicted in a movie or in real life.

So, this brings us back to the original premise of this blog, people are being taken to task for what they've done that has hurt other people. If any of the people involved had some personal realization in the past—realizing that what they had done was wrong, and said they were sorry and tried correct their past bad actions, they would probably not be in the cross hairs today. But, they did not. They did not care, they did not change, and they continued to embrace a mindset of hurt, damage, and destruction. Thus and therefore, they find themselves were they are today.

We can all learn from this. …Those of us who have hurt other people and did not listen to the pain we created, those of us who lie to ourselves and pretend we've done nothing wrong, and even those of us who have hurt no one. …We can learn hurt, hurts so we should never do it and never embrace those who do. For sooner or later, no matter how powerful we become, we all meet with our deserved fate.

The Things I Don't Want To Be
03/Jun/2018 06:27 PM

Life is an interesting adventure. We are tossed into this mess and we swim our way through it as best as we can. Some become great swimmer; they compete and they win. Others hate swimming all together but they have no choice, they have to keep on paddling or they will drown.

Some people are lucky and they find things that they really love to do with their life. They do them until they can do them no more. For most of us, however, we are doomed to do what we are forced to do for what other choice do we have, as we have to survive.

Every now and then I am reminded of how people view my life and myself and I am just amazed at how wrong they are. Because I have lived much of my life marginally in the public eye, people have often thrown their judgment about me and what I do my direction; both in a positive and a negative manner. But, they are more often than not totally wrong about who I am, why I do what I do, and what actually motivates me. Do they care they are wrong? Nope. Did they ever ask me anything? Nope. But, that's just life, people want to think what they think they know but they never truly know.

Back in the days when poetry actually mattered, when there was a culture behind it, and there was a lot of poetry being written and a lot chapbooks being published, for my poetry writing bio I would say, *"Former Swami, Former Punk Rocker, Former Ph.D."* And, that's how I saw myself. I still do. As I did then and I do now, when asked about my college degrees I say, *"They've expired..."*

As for being a sannyasin in India, if haven't been there doing that, you have no idea. If you have not possessed the mindset to live that lifestyle, you can and will never understand. But, I left it behind.

A lot of people see me as a martial artist due to the tons and tons of stuff I have written. When I first started out, it was fun. I had a story to tell. Then it got so trying and the mags and the publishers really pay for shit. It was just not worth it. But, all of the editors kept contacting me. It was kind of like that scene in the Godfather Part Three when Al Pacino's character says, *"I keep trying to get out but they keep dragging me back in."* There came a time when I just didn't want to do it any more. But, they wouldn't let me go. They kept asking for more. They wanted to bank on my skillset and my name. They wanted to do that but give me nothing in return.

And the movies... Forget about it. Everybody thinks they know why I did what I did and do what I do. But, they have no idea. Virtually everything everyone has said about my filmmaking style is totally self-motivated and just flat out wrong. Like I always say, *"I'm alive! Here I am!"* But, nobody ever asks me anything. They just talk and critique. But, they get it wrong!

As for the people who have wanted to be a part of the film industry, got in touch with me, and I have taken under my wing, most have been less than thankful. Now, that is not true for all of them. There are a couple of people who we had and have a great working relationship. But, most are so lost in

196

their egos that if I said or did something they didn't like or someone said something negative about their performance or the film itself after the fact, all they could do was spew negativity about me. This, when I was the only one to ever give them a break. Look at the resumes of most of the people who have worked for me. It goes to the case in point that I was the only one who ever gave them a chance. If they had stayed around, they would have continued to work. But, because no one else would give them the time of day, their film career was over. And, I'm the bad guy?

You know, to the world of trolls out there, I can say, *"You should really be ashamed of yourself. What have you accomplished?"* I would also say, like I always say, *"They're the ones talking about me, I not the one talking about them."* But, do they read this blog? Probably not. If they did would they be whole enough to understand that they've made a mistake and admit it? Hell no. They just want to talk and they do not have enough self-respect to acknowledge that they may have been wrong, nor do they have enough going on in their own life to talk about themselves so they look to people like me as a topic for conversation.

Now, it is essential to note, this is not a blog based upon negativity. It is just a wake up call. I am telling you that you do not know who I am or why I do what I do. So, why are you talking about me? If you do not know who I am, do you know anything about anybody else? If you don't, why say a word? Moreover, if you cannot be strong enough to strike back at people who say negative things about other people, what does that say about your character?

197

To know me is to love me. But, you don't know me. :-)

*　　*　　*

How often do you take yourself outside of yourself and think about the other person first?

You Have Got To Care About People!
01/Jun/2018 02:49 PM

I stopped off at my local Starbucks this afternoon to grab a latte. The young barista who was at the counter had apparently just scalded his thumb with some boiling hot water and I could tell he was a bit confused about what to do. *"Put some ice on it,"* I told him. So he grabbed a cup of ice water and stuck his thumb in it. I told him he should really get out of there and go to the doctor or something. The other barista who was making the drinks told him to get back on the cash register and take my order. I told him, *"Don't worry about it. Take care of yourself."* But, he soldiered on and took my order.

As I was waiting for my drink, the shift-lead walked out of the bathroom, where she was apparently training this new, young, very pretty barista it how to do the Starbuck's whatever. I told her about the situation and that she should go and help out the guy and let him go home or something. She completely dismissed my words and made light of the whole situation. I told her, *"Wow, I don't want to be your friend..."* Then, she went into a whole discourse about how many times she had burned herself and how it was just part of the job, etc... *"You have got to care about people,"* I exclaimed.

And, this is the thing about life; you really need to care about people. It doesn't matter if you know them or not; you need to care! Without caring you have nothing.

I get it, there's a lot of people out there who are very self-involved, don't give a damn about anybody unless they give a damn about them, and try to cast shade whenever they have a chance. But, all of that does nothing for anybody! Think about it, what did not caring ever get you? Did it ever make anything in your life any better? But, what about when you cared? Even if you helped somebody just a little bit, everything was better.

Life is life and we all get burned sometimes. If there is no one there to lend a helping hand, what does it all mean? You have got to care about people!

Everybody's Talking
About What Other People Are Saying
01/Jun/2018 07:54 AM

It seems that we have entered into a new era where everybody has something to say about what someone else has said. First of all... I guess this is based in the fact that so many people have so many ways to say nothing of any value. Twitter is a big culprit because it is so instantaneous. People don't think before they do. But, there are many other platforms, as well.

You know, we all have these thoughts that pass through our brains. As most people do not choose to follow a path of refined consciousness, the majority of all of the world's populous just allow themselves to spurt out whatever comes to mind. If they love something, hate something, or really have no factual idea of what they are talking about, nothing stops them, they just say what they say, consequences be damned.

Certainly, what happened to Rosanne and the instantaneous cancellation of her show a few days ago is an idea example. ...A TV show that was the number one rated show on the ABC network. It didn't matter. She crossed a line by what she tweeted and the show was pulled. I think they said that two hundred people instantly lost their jobs due to her one tweet. What is the karma for that?

Sure, she said it was an Ambien based tweet. But, no matter what drug you are taking, prescribed or otherwise, you only say what you are thinking.

Now, a lot of trolls are out there are spouting all kinds of untruths, lies, nonsense, personally motivate idioms, and the like. Most of the people are too meaningless to even use their real names. But, whether a person hides behind a screen name or uses their given name there are all kinds of foul, negative things being said. But, do any of these people question why they are doing it and to what end? I mean, I imagine Rosanne said what she said based upon a combination of being an outspoken comedian and holding certain thoughts and ideologies about certain people in her mind.

Side Note: Have you ever spent any time hanging out with a comedian? If they are full-bore into their craft, these people never turn off. They are on, talking all the time. That's way so many of them end up either under the care of a shrink or spending some serious time in a psych ward. They don't posses the boundaries that most of us are defined by. So, they are constantly letting loose. And, this is not a good place to exist within. Anyway…

We all think and believe what we think and believe. But, it is how we arrived at those conclusions and what we do with that information once we have arrived at it that defines us as a person.

Have you ever thought something about a person and then when you got to know them you realized you were totally wrong? Have you ever heard something about someone or something and when you investigated the subject on you own you realized what you were told was totally wrong? Have you ever taken the time to question why you think what you think and how will what you do, based upon what you think, affect you, the life of another person, or the greater world as a whole?

What you think matters. Why you think what you think matters. What you say, based upon what you think, matters. It matters because it can affect a whole lot of people. If you don't care about this fact, if you say and do everything based upon the nothingness of your own undefined sentiments, you have done nothing but hurt yourself as you have damage a lot of the everything else.

Now, I am sure there is a certain subset of Americas who were all about what Rosanne said. ... Liked it, thought it was funny, and agreed with it. I'm sure some were even stoked by and invigorated by her words of negativity. But, if the only way you can find some internal joy is to say something negative about someone else or believe something negative based upon what someone else has said, you really need to take a look at your life.

Consciousness is about making everything better in any way that you can, even if you don't like someone or something. Unconsciousness is about damage. And, damage not only hurts other people but will come back to hurt you. All actions are never ending. They always return to the person who instigated them.

So, stop negativity in it source. Stop it in you. Even if you believe you are responding to a negative action that you feel was done to you, be more than the instigator and meet all negativity with positivity. For that is how you live a good and conscious life and actually make the world a better place.

31/May/2018 04:35 PM

What if what you are saying is wrong?

What if what you are saying is a lie?

What if what you are saying hurts someone?

What if people believe what you are saying that is wrong, a lie, or hurts someone?

Where does the karma end?

31/May/2018 12:12 PM

Does saying something negative about another person make you a better person?

Does saying something negative about another person make them a worse person?

We should all define our lives by what makes us, other people, and the whole world better.

Negativity never achieves that goal.

29/May/2018 06:41 PM

Just because you say something with a smile on your face does not make it right.

If what you are saying is hurting anyone, what you are saying is wrong.

Don't support people who attack other people by saying bad things.

Nice People Aren't at the Top
29/May/2018 08:39 AM

When you look at your life where do you find yourself? Do you find yourself fulfilled? Do you find yourself content? Do you find yourself supporting yourself in an adequate manner?

When you look at your life who are you reliant upon? Who do you need in your life to maintain your level of survival and to continue living the life you have become accustomed to? Is your life, your finances, and your living situation in a state of stability or can it all easily fall away from you?

When you look at your life who do you turn to for guidance? Do you look to your family, your friend, a religious leader, or are you completely self-contained? Do you only ask yourself what you should do and do you only blame yourself for any mistakes that you make? Or, do you continually turn the blame elsewhere.

Life is a complex web of interpersonal relationships based upon human needs. Why we do what we decide to do can be defined by many ideologies and philosophies but at best, they are only a guess, for what a person ultimate does is only truly demarcated by what that person does. They are the only one who truly knows why. But they only know if they take the time to analysis and develop an answer to that question.

Once a person does what they do, (once any of us do what we do), then the rest of our life and our life choices are set into motion. Most people don't think about this, however. They just do. They just are influenced into doing something, told that they should do something, and/or do what they do because it feels good. From this, absolute destiny is set into motion.

Some people, for whatever reason, find their way to a position of power. They either see a goal and work towards it or that position is handed to them. Sometimes, it is a little bit of both. Once they have arrived at that position of power, it causes them to take action and do things that will affect the life of other people. From this, they either do things that helps other people or they do things that hurts other people. Sometimes, the same action has a different effect on two separate individuals. Yet, it was one person doing one thing that helped, hurt, guided, or lead another human astray.

How many people attain where they are in life and truly understand why they have arrived there? How many people once they have arrived care that the influence that they have may truly change the life or another person? What they say, what they do, what they feel while doing what they do, all has consequence. But, are they aware enough of this fact to cause them to truly think before the do? Or, do they just do, motivated by an individualized desire to gain or maintain power, control, and/or continued fulfillment of their desires?

Recently, I watched the Netflix documentary, *"Wild, Wild Country,"* about the spiritual leader Bhagwan Shree Rajneesh and his foremost disciple of the time Ma Anand Sheela. Though it was six hours in length and as a filmmaker I found it to be a bit long-winded, it truly

209

provides a microscope into the complex psychology of power and how a person acts once they possess said power.

As the TV news anchors say, *"Full disclosure,"* I must tell you, I spent time with and was initiated by Bhagwan Shree Rajneesh in India in the 1970s. This documentary primarily focuses on the time when the group purchased a ranch in Oregon, which from the moment it happened I knew was a big mistake. Though Oregon sometimes has a description as being a bit of a hippie oasis, it is far more inhabited by rednecks than hippies. That was one of the group's primary mistakes. Had they located in California, none of the ensuing destiny would have manifested.

When I was with Rajneesh in India, it was a very different time from when they arrived on the farm in Oregon. It was all about embracing freedom. For many of us who were there at that time and had been schooled in the realms of restrictive eastern metaphysics where celibacy and formal seated meditation was propagated, it opened a new window into reality and a redefining of true spirituality. It was great! He truly was a spiritual revolutionary.

Did I think he was the second-coming or anything like that, as some people did? No. He was just a man who presented a new take on the road to enlightenment. But, like all spiritual teachers I had met and have studied with, I saw his flaws. Everybody has them. But, it was not Rajneesh, himself, that caused me to leave his fold. Whereas in regard to my years with Swami Satchidananda, it was more the people that were in a position of power that caused me to leave the group. In Rajneesh India, it was more the uncontrolled chaos defined by people that were in need of a father figure or who weren't really there for enlightenment but simply wanted easy sex and wild non-stop partying, all placed under the guise of spirituality. For me, I was about nirvana, not just another orgasms.

I never visited Rajneesh or the commune in Oregon. I had gained all I could from his teaching in India. But, to watch the documentary it was truly revealing about why people do what they do and what motivates them. If you can sit through it and keep an open mind, you can really witness a lot about the concept of human power and the cost thereof. You will see how Ma Anand Sheela, this charismatic figurehead, truly guided the community to... Well, I'll let you decide... And, how the people who occupied powerful position in the U.S. government did what they did with absolute power while possessing no inner understanding of who or what they were dealing with.

And, to the source point of this blog, this is where all the problems with personal power, merging with a group consciousness, emerge. There is one person who has a vision and from that one person either great good is created or great bad is instigated. And sometimes, in the early stages, it is hard to see which is which.

So, as you pass though life, study who holds the power over you. Study who you allow to hold the power over you. Study why you do what you do because of what someone, who holds the power over you, asks you to do. But, more than all that, know yourself. Always question why you are doing what you are doing. Know the reason why. From this, even though there may be people in a position of power who overshadow your existence, you can stay true to yourself, doing things that only help people and hurts no one. Then, at the end of your days, you will know that there is no one to blame but yourself.

Confronting the Confronters
26/May/2018 07:10 AM

There are a lot of stupid people out there who say a lot of stupid things. Probably all of us, at one time or another, have fallen into this category. This doesn't make it right; it just makes it a fact of life. But, for most of us, we try to be more. The problem is, there are a lot of people saying a lot of stupid stuff out there that raises our blood pressure, gets us mad, and so we respond. This is the wrong thing to do, however. For all that does is give these people power.

On Facebook they sometimes show how some person goes on a racist rant against another person—makes some stupid racist remark, which then causes the person who the remarks were made against to get mad, turn on their camera, and say something back at them. Sometimes it turns into a fight. But, if you step back from this situation, look at it from a clearer perspective, and watch the instigator, that is exactly what they want. They have won. They said what they were feeling. They obviously hurt the person they were trying to insult, which then lead to a confrontation. So what that you put them on YouTube and make them look stupid. They said what they felt and that is all that matters to them. You're not going to change their mind. They are not, all of a sudden, going to say, *"You're right. I'm' wrong. I'm sorry for being a racist. I will change."*

It is like Spike Lee recently went on this rant about Donald Trump at Cann. It was all, *"That mutha fucka this, that mutha facka that."* All it did was to make Spike Lee look bad. Not only does speaking like that (particularly in a public setting) bring down your creditability as a human being, but it just makes you (anyone) look bad. If you have something say, and we all do, say it with dignity, then people might listen.

Racism and rants go on all over the place. I've recently talked about this in a blog and discussed how I grew up in an African-American neighborhood experiencing racism from a Caucasian perspective. The sad thing was, my childhood lived in that manner, indoctrinated me into believing that is how people are suppose to communicate. But, that is just wrong. You need to be able to rise yourself above that level of interaction. But, you see it all the time. Somebody cuts somebody off when they're driving, if that person is of a different race, the first words out of their mouth are, *"You whatever..."* A couple years ago when I was driving in South L.A. I was surprised when a young African-American man cut me off and then said, *"You white mutha fucka."* Wow... It's still going on...

The fact is, it goes on everywhere on every level. Not long ago I walked into a store with my lady and one of the young African-American cashiers said out loud, *"It's John and Yoko."* Now, there was a part in my that got really pissed off at what he said. And, I could have taken it to the next level like the aforementioned people do. But, what would it have proven? It was just a mindless person making a stupid comment based upon a misaligned mindset.

But, this all goes to the point... There are stupid people out there who say stupid things. Don't let them drag you into their melodrama! Be more. Meet negativity with positivity. Then, maybe everything will become just a little bit better.

25/May/2018 01:51 PM

When you stare out across the horizon are you enthralled by what you see or are you locked into the thoughts that are already in your head?

I went to this café I like for breakfast this morning. As I was walking towards the door a lady rushes through it in front of me. That's fine. It made me smile.

Inside, the lady walks up to the counter and start looking at the bakery items and asking questions about the menu. Questions answered, she stood there apparently making up her mind for a very-very-very long period of time.

The cashier, who I know, rolled her eyes. She and I smiled back and forth as the lady stood there blocking any progress of any moving forward for myself or for the line of people that had formed behind me. Completely oblivious, the lady did not order, she just stood there staring at the menu. Finally, another employee, noticing the situation, stepped up to the counter to take my order at another cash register.

I'm sure we have all experienced situations like this in our lives. …An oblivious person, completely blocking any forward movement in our existence. Is it that they are simply unaware or is it that they somehow find empowerment in behaving in this manner? I don't know? I guess each person has his or her own psychological motivations. But, the fact of the matter is, when someone acts like this they imped the progress of another person's life. They put the breaks on reality.

In life, I believe that it is really important that we each check our review mirror. To claim to live a life of caring consciousness, we must know

217

what is taking place in our wake—who we are affecting behind us and how what we have previously done is impacting the lives of those that our action(s) have impacted.

Everybody can claim, *"I didn't know,"* as an excuse. But, an excuse is all that it is for, *"Not knowing,"* is only illustrating that you don't care enough to know.

Think about other people as you live your life. Think about how what you are doing is affecting them. Care.

The Power That You Feel
25/May/2018 07:43 AM

The majority of life's people exist in a space where they do not seek power, control, or dominance over any one or any thing. They simply hope to live their life as best as they can. As they exist in a space of doing what they are doing; i.e. going to work to raise their family and the like, the concept of expansive power never comes to mind. They just live. And, this is a good thing. They do what humanity is supposed to do; exist.

There is, however, another breed of person who seeks dominance, control, and power over other people. The people who embody this mindset come to this delineation via various methods. Some actually seek it out while others simply happen into it. However one arrives at obtaining a position where they possess the ability to exercise control over another person, it is there that they find the ability to invoke prodigious good or abundant evil.

If we look around in this current day, there are a number of people at the forefront of the news who, from a position of power, have done some very bad things. There are the film industry executives and the famous players, the self-help group that turned into a sex cult, and the religious leaders who have fallen from grace and used their power to gain their deviant desires; whatever those desires may be. And, these are just the people in the news. There are so many more people, at so many levels, throughout the spectrum of life, that use their power to influence and control other people that it is almost unfathomable. Perhaps it is the boss who is full of himself or herself and dominates their employees in a negative manner. Maybe it is the Instagram or YouTube personality who guides people down a road that is dominated solely by their own personal perspective on reality, equaling a way for them to make money. Maybe it is the heckler in the audience who does not let the performer perform and continues to harass their show. And, the list goes on. There are people who find some source of power at some level of life and use it draw attention to themselves and from this attention gain control over the thoughts and actions of others.

Some people set out to gain a position of power. Many, however, just happen into it. In either case, once they have arrived, it is what they do with that power that sets the stage for their life and the lives of all they influence due to the authority they wield.

A good percentage of the people that hold onto the reins of power do so from a completely unconscious and irreverent perspective. They have the ability to guide the thoughts and the lives of people, yet they only tell people what they, personally, believe and from this they create a following that emanates their same thought process. This is dangerous. For this is where cults are born. One person at the top guiding others down the road to damnation.

The biggest problem is the invocation of a person who holds power is that this power becomes very addicting. They have people listening to them. They have people believing in them. They have people supporting them; emotionally and financially. Thus, they become absorbed with the power they hold and this is where all of the problems of life begin. This is where all of those who are currently in the news have found the impetus for the bad deeds they have instigated.

So, what does this tell us about life? It tells us that some people obtain a position of power by one method or another. From this, they hold sway over other people. If what they do with this power is wholly good it would be hard to find fault with their actions. But, if their words and their actions guide others to do things against their own will or to believe things that are not valid, equaling the damaging of anyone else's life, then the power they have is one of the source points for all of the bad of the world. And, this is not good.

What can you do? Sometimes you are forced to listen to a person in a position of power: i.e. your teacher, your boss, your police, or your politicians. That is just a fact of life. But, then there are the other people. The people who are promising you a something. The people who are guiding you based upon nothing more than their own interpretation of the scriptures or life. Why give them the power? Why choose to relinquish your own mind and your own ability to make your own choices? Sure, it is easier to just be told what to think, what to do, and why you should think and do it. But, this what these people thrive on. And, from this, all you do is to put the power into another person's hands and from this you allow them to control you and other people.

If you give a person the power, they will take the power. Keep the power for yourself. Think for yourself and then your world is your world.

221

The Good That You Do
24/May/2018 07:25 PM

Everybody knows what is good. When you see it, when you hear it, when you experience it, you know that it is good. It makes whomever it encounters better.

Some people try to do good. Some people strive to do good. Some people turn off their egos and go out of their way to do good. Do you?

Just as everyone immediately know what it is good; everyone immediately knows what is bad. Hurting anyone or anything for any reason is bad.

But, there is commonly a place where the definition of good and bad becomes convoluted. Though they should not, they do. Why do they? Because some people become motivated by their own desired outcome and from this they place their own definition and rational upon their actions. Though their actions may, in fact, be bad and/or harmful, they are presented as being good.

The definition of bad is obvious. But, do you think about this definition before you decide to do what you do or say what you say? Judgment or criticism are two of the most obvious and commonplace forms of badness that are presented and believed to be good. But, they hurt people, so by their very definition they are bad.

Projecting personal beliefs onto a particular subject or person is also oftentimes presented as being good when it is anything but. The question you have to ask yourself is, *"Who is believing what you are believing? Is it everyone or is it simply you having concocted an ideology in your own mind*

222

which causes you to present it to the world with the hopes that others will believe as you do?" Again, as this behavior has the potential of negatively affecting the lives of other people, there is no goodness in your actions.

All good things and all bad things boil down to what one person does. What do you do? Do you allow your ego, your cultural programing, and your projected desires to guide you to do what you do? If you do, then how can what you are doing be universally seen as being good?

Doing good helps one person or it helps everyone. Doing bad hurts one person or it hurts everyone. Can you be whole enough to always do good? If you can—if no one is hurt by your actions, then everything, everywhere becomes just a little bit better.

Strive to do good.

Throw a Pillow Instead of a Punch
23/May/2018 07:34 AM

You don't like someone. Your dislike for them causes you to take action. Your action causes you to do or say something negative about that person. What occurs from this action? As you have damaged the life of that person, you have instigated negative karma that will be redirected towards you.

Before you feel anything, before you do anything, do you ever look deeply within yourself and question why you are feeling what you are feeling towards that person and why those feelings are causing you to take action?

You like someone. Your affection for them causes you to take action. Your action causes you to do or to say something positive about that person. What occurs from this action? As you have helped the life of that person, you have instigated positive karma that will be redirected towards you.

Before you feel anything, before you do anything, do you ever look deeply within yourself and question why you are feeling what you are feeling towards that person and why those feelings are causing you to take action?

Life is a process of action and evolution based upon emotions. Emotions emanate from within each person. What a person feels is what causes them to act. But, every action equals a reaction. If you hurt, you will be hurt. If you help, you will be help. It is a very simple equation. Most people don't think about this before they do, however. Most people never peel back the layers and get down to the root source of their feelings and why they are feeling what they feel, causing them to do what they do. From this, they either spread negativity, causing them to live a life defined by ongoing negativity or they spread positivity, causing them to live a life defined by ongoing positivity.

If you don't know why you do what you do, then you just act. Undefined action leads to nothing more than a life framed by undefined chaos; be that chaos based upon negativity or positivity.

If you think you know why you feel what you feel about a person or about anything else for that matter and you want to use those feelings to be a causation factor for taking action, do you ever calculate the consequences of that action on the life of that other person or onto the anything else before you instigate that action? Again, if you don't know, you don't know. If you don't know or you don't care all that creates is the implementation of a negative action, as someone will be negativity affected by what you are planning to do, if what you are planning to do has no basis in a calculated outcome.

If you want to live a good life, do good things and say good things. If you want to live a life defined by chaos and confusion, do the opposite.

All things you choose to do will come back to you. Therefore, know why you are doing what you are doing. Understand the consequences not only to whom you are doing it to but to you for doing it in the first place.

Karma is Real
22/May/2018 07:10 AM

Twenty or twenty-five years ago I used to be asked to write a lot of articles about the advanced metaphysical aspects of karma from a Hindu perspective. You can read one of those essays over on the Human Consciousness page of this website if you feel like it. I don't know that the interest in the subject of karma has really changed that much over the years but it seems that as the understanding has become fairly commonplace; delving deeper into this understanding has waned.

This being said, karma is real. What you do causes the next set of experiences you will experience to be set into motion. If you help one person, you help the whole world. If you hurt one person, you hurt the whole world. But, it seems that so many people are so lost in the action of doing that they do not consider this fact.

One of the great things about age and getting older is that you get to view things through the perspective of time. You get to witness how certain people's lives evolve based upon what they have done.

For example, I have watched as some people have risen literally to the top of the world. They got there by using people and their creations to arrive at that level. And, they fucked everyone over on their way to the top. I have witnessed this particularly in the film industry. The higher they rose, the more they surrounded themselves with cronies and attorneys in an effort to kept doing what they were doing and to kept their lifestyle vibrant. They did this until it all feel apart. Then, they ended up with literally nothing. The stories I could tell you...

For most people it is not like that, however. Most people will never have the drive and the uncaring desire to achieve that level of life and lifestyle. And, that's a good thing. But, that is not to say that many people do not follow a similar path of selfish, hurtful activity; it is simply defined by a smaller standard.

For most who enact bad karma, they are not even consciously aware enough to care what they are doing. They are just doing, motivated by the, *"Whatever,"* mindset. The most common reason for behaving in this manner is that their life is in such a state of unfulfilled chaos that they simply live a life based upon emotional reaction. They think, they feel, they do, but they do not consciously consider what they do. From this, many people never raise their life above the level they currently inhibit. Their entire life definition is based upon chaos and reactive destruction.

For each of these aforementioned mindsets you are not going to be able to tell these people that karma is real and it is coming. For the first, they are too driven by their ego and/or the financial gratification they are receiving. For the ladder, they are just lost in undefined anger and/or the need to lash out due to their own sense of unfulfilled desire. Thus, they want to hurt anyone they can focus their attention upon.

But, where does this leave us? It leaves us at the root source of why some people hurt, why so many people rise and then have a terrible fall, and why so many lives are hurt or damaged by the

227

actions of another person. People don't think. People don't care. People just do until they can do no longer.

If you are motivated to say something bad about, do something bad to, take something from, or hurt another person in any way, do you ever question your motivations? Do you ever take the time to get to the root of your emotions and why you want to behave in that manner, towards that person, in the first place? Do you ever question how you would feel if it was done to you?

I think we all have had something done to us, by someone else, that has hurt us or hurt our life. I would imagine that most of us have done things that have hurt another person or their life, as well. But, it is whom we are on the inside that then dictates how we will react and what we will do next.

First of all, do you ever watch your own karma? Do you ever do something and then take notice of what happens next? Maybe it isn't the next day, the next week, or even the next year, but do you ever get counterpunched by life and then realize, *"I know why that happened."* Most people don't. They don't think about those things. They just become upset at the fact that something happened to them that they did not like and then they become upset. But, if you don't look to your past, if you don't study what you have done and what was the reaction, then you will never understand the true science of karma and life.

All life comes down to you. All life comes down to what you do. All life comes down to how you treat other people. You want to know what is coming next in your life, critically study your life and the karmic answer will be revealed.

Karma is real.

FADE OUT.

THE ZEN